MANUFACTURING AUTOMATION

AUTHOR

Dr. Chitragupt Swaroop Chitransh

Assistant Professor

Department of Mechanical Engineering IMS Engineering College, Ghaziabad

REVIEWER

Dr. Mohd Javaid

Associate Professor

Department of Mechanical Engineering Jamia Millia Islamia, New Delhi

KHANNA BOOK PUBLISHING CO. (P) Ltd.
4C/4344, Ansari Road, Darya Ganj, New Delhi, India

All India Council for Technical Education
Nelson Mandela Marg, Vasant Kunj, New Delhi, India

Dear Readers,

To prevent the piracy, this book is secured with HIGH SECURITY HOLOGRAM on the front title cover. In case you don't find the hologram on the front cover title, please write us to at contact@khannabooks.com or whatsapp us at +91-99109 09320 and avail special gift voucher for yourself.

Specimen of Hologram on front Cover title:

Moreover, there is a SPECIAL DISCOUNT COUPON for you with EVERY HOLOGRAM.

How to avail this SPECIAL DISCOUNT:

Step 1: Scratch the hologram

Step 2: Under the scratch area, your "coupon code" is available

Step 3: Logon to www.khannabooks.com

Step 4: Use your "coupon code" in the shopping cart and get your copy at a special discount

Step 5: Enjoy your reading!

ISBN: 978-93-5538-841-4

Book Code: UG488EN

Manufacturing Automation

by Dr. Chitragupt Swaroop Chitransh

First Edition: 2026

Originally Published by:

All India Council for Technical Education, Ministry of Education, GOI

Exclusively Published & Distributed by:

Khanna Book Publishing Co. (P) Ltd.

4C/4344, Ansari Road, Daryaganj,
New Delhi (INDIA)

Visit us at: **www.khannabooks.com**

Write us at: **contact@khannabooks.com**

To view complete list of books, Please scan the QR Code:

KPH

Printed in Bharat.

प्रो. टी. जी. सीताराम
अध्यक्ष
Prof. T. G. Sitharam
Chairman

सत्यमेव जयते

आज़ादी का अमृत महोत्सव

अखिल भारतीय तकनीकी शिक्षा परिषद्
(भारत सरकार का एक सांविधिक निकाय)
(शिक्षा मंत्रालय, भारत सरकार)
नेल्सन मंडेला मार्ग, वसंत कुंज, नई दिल्ली–110070
दूरभाष : 011–26131498
ई–मेल : chairman@aicte-india.org

ALL INDIA COUNCIL FOR TECHNICAL EDUCATION
(A STATUTORY BODY OF THE GOVT. OF INDIA)
(Ministry of Education, Govt. of India)
Nelson Mandela Marg, Vasant Kunj, New Delhi-110070
Phone : 011-26131498
E-mail : chairman@aicte-india.org

FOREWORD

Engineers are the backbone of any modern society. They are the ones responsible for the marvels as well as the improved quality of life across the world. Engineers have driven humanity towards greater heights in a more evolved and unprecedented manner.

The All India Council for Technical Education (AICTE), have spared no efforts towards the strengthening of the technical education in the country. AICTE is always committed towards promoting quality Technical Education to make India a modern developed nation emphasizing on the overall welfare of mankind.

An array of initiatives has been taken by AICTE in last decade which have been accelerated now by the National Education Policy (NEP) 2020. The implementation of NEP under the visionary leadership of Hon'ble Prime Minister of India envisages the provision for education in regional languages to all, thereby ensuring that every graduate becomes competent enough and is in a position to contribute towards the national growth and development through innovation & entrepreneurship.

One of the spheres where AICTE had been relentlessly working since past couple of years is providing high quality original technical contents at Under Graduate & Diploma level prepared and translated by eminent educators in various Indian languages to its aspirants. For students pursuing 2nd year of their Engineering education, AICTE has identified 87 books, which shall be translated into 12 Indian languages - Hindi, Tamil, Gujarati, Odia, Bengali, Kannada, Urdu, Punjabi, Telugu, Marathi, Assamese & Malayalam. In addition to the English medium, books in different Indian Languages are going to support the students to understand the concepts in their respective mother tongue.

On behalf of AICTE, I express sincere gratitude to all distinguished authors, reviewers and translators from the renowned institutions of high repute for their admirable contribution in a record span of time.

AICTE is confident that these outcomes based original contents shall help aspirants to master the subject with comprehension and greater ease.

(Prof. T. G. Sitharam)

ACKNOWLEDGEMENT

The authors are grateful to the authorities of AICTE, particularly Prof. T. G. Sitharam, Chairman; Dr. Abhay Jere, Vice-Chairman; Prof. Rajiv Kumar, Member-Secretary, Dr. Ramesh Unnikrishnan, Advisor-II and Dr. Sunil Luthra, Director, Training and Learning or their planning to publish the books on ***Manufacturing Automation***.

I sincerely acknowledge the valuable contributions of the reviewer of the book Prof. (Dr.) Mohd Javaid, Associate professor, Jamia Millia Islamia, Prof. (Dr.) Arvinder Kaur, Dean USAR GGSIPU Delhi, Prof. (Dr.) Ajay Singholi, Professor, USAR GGSIPU Delhi, Prof. (Dr.) Vikram Bali, Director, IMS Engineering College Ghaziabad, Prof. (Dr.) Ravi Dwivedi, Professor, MANIT Bhopal, Dr. Vivek Pandey, HOD, IMS Engineering College Ghaziabad, Mr. Manish Kumar, Assistant Professor, IMS Engineering College Ghaziabad. I am also thankful to my mother Asha Khare, my father Vijay Kumar Khare, my wife Srishti Khare; my son Daivik Khare, my brother Vishnu and my nephew Vedik Khare, as without their support, this work would not have come to fruition.

I would also like to acknowledge the reference books that have been instrumental in the preparation of this book: " Automation, Production Systems and Computer-integrated Manufacturing " by M. P. Groover; “Manufacturing - Engineering and Technology” by S. Kalpakjian and S. R. Schmid; “Computer Control of Manufacturing Systems; by Yoram Koren; "CAD/CAM Principles and Applications" by P.N. Rao. Additionally, I extend my gratitude to my students, over the years, who have made significant contributions that have enriched my experience and expertise in this subject. I am immensely grateful for their valuable input for making this book students’ friendly and giving a better shape in an artistic manner.

This book is an outcome of various suggestions of AICTE members, experts and authors who shared their opinion and thought to further develop the engineering education in our country. Acknowledgements are due to the contributors and different workers in this field whose published books, review articles, papers, photographs, footnotes, references and other valuable information enriched us at the time of writing the book.

Dr. Chitragupt Swaroop Chitransh

PREFACE

Welcome to the world of manufacturing automation! This book includes the topics recommended by AICTE, in a very systematic and orderly manner serves as your comprehensive guide to understanding the principles, concepts, and applications of digital electronics. Whether you are a student embarking on a journey of learning or a professional seeking to refresh your knowledge, this book is designed to provide you with a solid foundation in this fascinating field.

Manufacturing automation has revolutionized the way we live, work, and communicate. From the automobiles we rely on to the computers that power our daily tasks, manufacturing automation form the backbone of modern technology. Understanding the fundamentals of manufacturing automation is crucial for anyone involved in fields such as mechanical engineering, computer engineering, robotics, and information technology.

In this book, we will embark on a journey that will take us through the intricacies of manufacturing automation, automated assembly analysis, and design. We will explore the building blocks of manufacturing automation, including Automation scalability, Design and analysis of automated flow lines, digital, inclusive, smart and distributed manufacturing etc. We will delve into the world of manufacturing automation, understanding how to analyse, design, and automated assembly systems.

Throughout the chapters, we will emphasize a hands-on approach to learning. We will provide practical examples, step-by-step explanations, and opportunities for you to apply your knowledge through exercises and projects. We will not only focus on the theoretical aspects of manufacturing automation but also explore its practical applications. From manufacturing automation, we will uncover how manufacturing automation plays a vital role in various domains.

As you progress through this book, we encourage you to actively engage with the material, ask questions, and seek deeper understanding. manufacturing automation can sometimes be challenging, but with perseverance and practice, you will gain the necessary skills to analyse, design, and troubleshoot automated flow lines for manufacturing with confidence.

We would like to express our gratitude to the countless researchers, educators, and engineers who have contributed to the field of manufacturing automation over the years. Their collective efforts have paved the way for the advancements we witness today. We hope that this book will serve as a tribute to their contributions and inspire you to further explore the exciting possibilities of manufacturing automation.

We sincerely hope that this book will be a valuable resource in your journey of learning and discovery. We invite you to immerse yourself in the world of manufacturing automation and embark on an adventure that will empower you to shape the future.

Happy reading! Happy Learning!

Dr. Chitragupt Swaroop Chitransh

OUTCOME BASED EDUCATION

For the implementation of an outcome-based education the first requirement is to develop an outcome-based curriculum and incorporate an outcome-based assessment in the education system. By going through outcome-based assessments evaluators will be able to evaluate whether the students have achieved the outlined standard, specific and measurable outcomes. With the proper incorporation of outcome-based education there will be a definite commitment to achieve a minimum standard for all learners without giving up at any level. At the end of the programme running with the aid of outcome-based education, a student will be able to arrive at the following outcomes:

PO1. Engineering knowledge: Apply the knowledge of mathematics, science, engineering fundamentals, and an engineering specialization to the solution of complex engineering problems.

PO2. Problem analysis: Identify, formulate, review research literature, and analyze complex engineering problems reaching substantiated conclusions using first principles of mathematics, natural sciences, and engineering sciences.

PO3. Design / development of solutions: Design solutions for complex engineering problems and design system components or processes that meet the specified needs with appropriate consideration for the public health and safety, and the cultural, societal, and environmental considerations.

PO4. Conduct investigations of complex problems: Use research-based knowledge and research methods including design of experiments, analysis and interpretation of data, and synthesis of the information to provide valid conclusions.

PO5. Modern tool usage: Create, select, and apply appropriate techniques, resources, and modern engineering and IT tools including prediction and modelling to complex engineering activities with an understanding of the limitations.

PO6. The engineer and society: Apply reasoning informed by the contextual knowledge to assess societal, health, safety, legal and cultural issues and the consequent responsibilities relevant to the professional engineering practice.

PO7. Environment and sustainability: Understand the impact of the professional engineering solutions in societal and environmental contexts, and demonstrate the knowledge of, and need for sustainable development.

PO8. Ethics: Apply ethical principles and commit to professional ethics and responsibilities and norms of the engineering practice.

PO9. Individual and team work: Function effectively as an individual, and as a member or leader in diverse teams, and in multidisciplinary settings.

PO10. Communication: Communicate effectively on complex engineering activities with the engineering community and with society at large, such as, being able to comprehend and write effective reports and design documentation, make effective presentations, and give and receive clear instructions.

PO11. Project management and finance: Demonstrate knowledge and understanding of the engineering and management principles and apply these to one's own work, as a member and leader in a team, to manage projects and in multidisciplinary environments.

PO12. Life-long learning: Recognize the need for, and have the preparation and ability to engage in independent and life-long learning in the broadest context of technological change.

COURSE OUTCOMES

After completion of the course the students will be able to:

CO-1: Understand the fundamentals of automations and various numerical control machines, CNC basics and computer-aided process planning.

CO-2: Understand automated flow lines including various work part transport and transfer mechanisms, Feedback systems and control; Modular and reconfigurable machines, adaptive machine controls

CO-3: Become familiar with various Automated Assembly Systems and their characteristics, including transfer systems; vibratory and non-vibratory feeders; Feed tracks, part orienting and placing mechanisms

CO-4: Understand the Lean manufacturing, design and analysis of automated flow lines including average production time, production rate, line efficiency, analysis of transfer lines without storage, partial and full automation.

CO-5: Enhance their problem-solving and critical thinking abilities for Mechanical, electro-mechanical, pneumatic and hydraulic systems; Sensors integration; Process monitoring, data analysis and control using actuators; Robots.

CO-6: Learn about digital, inclusive, smart and distributed manufacturing, depending on the course, students might also explore recent trends in Industry 4.0; Digital transformations in shop-floors (CIM to Smart factory; Intelligent machines to Smart Machines; Factory automation to Distributed automation; Human sense to system sensed.

Course Outcomes	Expected Mapping with Programme Outcomes (1- Weak Correlation; 2- Medium correlation; 3- Strong Correlation)											
	PO-1	PO-2	PO-3	PO-4	PO-5	PO-6	PO-7	PO-8	PO-9	PO-10	PO-11	PO-12
CO-1	3	3	3	3	2	2	2	1	1	1	3	3
CO-2	3	3	3	3	2	2	2	1	1	1	3	3
CO-3	3	3	3	3	2	2	2	1	1	1	3	3
CO-4	3	3	3	3	2	2	2	1	1	1	3	3
CO-5	3	3	3	3	2	2	2	1	1	1	3	3
CO-6	3	3	3	3	2	2	2	1	1	1	3	3

GUIDELINES FOR TEACHERS

To implement Outcome Based Education (OBE) knowledge level and skill set of the students should be enhanced. Teachers should take a major responsibility for the proper implementation of OBE. Some of the responsibilities (not limited to) for the teachers in OBE system may be as follows:

- Within reasonable constraint, they should manoeuvre time to the best advantage of all students.
- They should assess the students only upon certain defined criterion without considering any other potential ineligibility to discriminate them.
- They should try to grow the learning abilities of the students to a certain level before they leave the institute.
- They should try to ensure that all the students are equipped with the quality knowledge as well as competence after they finish their education.
- They should always encourage the students to develop their ultimate performance capabilities.
- They should facilitate and encourage group work and team work to consolidate newer approach.
- They should follow Blooms taxonomy in every part of the assessment.

Bloom's Taxonomy

Level	Teacher should Check	Student should be able to	Possible Mode of Assessment
Create	Students' ability to create	Design or Create	Mini project
Evaluate	Students' ability to justify	Argue or Defend	Assignment
Analyze	Students' ability to distinguish	Differentiate or Distinguish	Project/Lab Methodology
Apply	Students' ability to use information	Operate or Demonstrate	Technical Presentation/ Demonstration
Understand	Students' ability to explain the ideas	Explain or Classify	Presentation/Seminar
Remember	Students' ability to recall (or remember)	Define or Recall	Quiz

GUIDELINES FOR STUDENTS

Students should take equal responsibility for implementing the OBE. Some of the responsibilities (not limited to) for the students in OBE system are as follows:

- Students should be well aware of each UO before the start of a unit in each and every course.
- Students should be well aware of each CO before the start of the course.
- Students should be well aware of each PO before the start of the programme.
- Students should think critically and reasonably with proper reflection and action.
- Learning of the students should be connected and integrated with practical and real life consequences.
- Students should be well aware of their competency at every level of OBE.

ABBREVIATIONS AND SYMBOLS

List of Abbreviations

Abbreviations	Full form	Abbreviations	Full form
CNC	Computer numerical control	NC	Numerical control
DNC	Direct numerical control	AI	Artificial Intelligence
CAPP	Computer aided process planning	DCS	Distributed control system
ROM	Read only memory	EDM	Electric discharge machine
W/S	Workstations	CIM	Computer integrated manufacturing
ML	Machine learning	IoT	Internet of Things
AGVs	Automated guided vehicles	CAD	Computer-aided design
CMM	Coordinate measuring machine	HMI	Human machine interfaces
GUIs	Graphical user interfaces	PLCs	Programmable logic controllers
DA	Distribution automation		

List of Symbols

Symbol	Symbol Name in Maths	Symbols Meaning	Example
V_{out}		Output voltage signals	
V_{in}		Input voltage	
T_{ic}	Ideal Cycle Time	Ideal cycle time on the line	$T_{ic} = T_{pr} + T_t$
T_{pr}		Processing time at station	
T_t		Transfer time	
F		Unplanned downtime Frequency	
$T_{p\text{-}average}$	Average production time	Actual average production time	$T_{p\text{-}average} = T_{ic} + F * T_{downtime}$
$T_{downtime}$		Downtime per line stop	

Symbol	Symbol Name in Maths	Symbols Meaning	Example
$R_{prod.}$		Production rate	
$T_{prod.}$		Production time	
R_{ic}		Ideal production rate	
T_c		Cycle time	
E		Line efficiency	

LIST OF FIGURES

CONTENTS

1 INTRODUCTION TO AUTOMATION

UNIT SPECIFICS

Understanding the processes and responsibilities associated with automation in industries begins with the introduction of automation. This chapter comprehensively overviews the fundamental principles and practices essential for effective automation.

RATIONALE

In automation industries, one must know about the processes, types and the elements of automation processes.

PRE-REQUISITE

Nil

UNIT OUTCOMES

List of outcomes of this unit is as follows:

U1-O1: Students should be able to understand the fundamentals of automation, specifically, the architecture, addressing modes and instruction set

U1-O2: Students should be able to brief CNC programming

U1-O3: Should be able to understand the fundamentals of computer aided process planning

Unit Outcomes	Expected Mapping with Programme Outcomes *(1- Weak Correlation; 2- Medium correlation; 3- Strong Correlation)*					
	PO-1	PO-2	PO-3	PO-4	PO-5	PO-6
U1-O1	3	1	3	1	1	2
U1-O2	3	1	2	2	2	3
U1-O3	3	2	2	1	1	2

An overview of the general framework and types of automation strategies that are commonly used in modern industries is presented in this chapter. This chapter describes the development and advancements in automation technology, specifically numerical control machines. It gives readers more information about the requirements for CNC programming as well as the benefits of these technologies in contemporary industry. The chapter's overview of automation, numerical control devices, and computer-aided process planning is its main section. It addresses the instruction set, addressing modes, and architecture. The principles of automation architecture, which are applied in industries based on plant layout and available space, are also covered in this chapter. Finally, a brief overview of computer-aided process planning and its features is provided at the end of the chapter.

1.1. Introduction of Automation

Automation has emerged as a critical component of manufacturing processes. Historically, production lead time and wage costs were key issues in the manufacturing sector. Later on, as technology and automated processes advanced, all of these difficulties and process challenges were minimized. Automation was introduced in the early 1940s, when the automobile industry extended its use of automation and control technologies in mechanical production lines. Automation technology has grown to the level that it has spawned a variety of new technologies, each with its own recognition and relevance.

It can be categorized as basic, process and intelligent automation. Basic automation involves automating simple, repetitive activities. This type of automation involves digitizing work and centralizing regular procedures, such as using one message platform rather than multiple channels. This lowers errors, speeds up transactions work, and allows individuals to focus on higher-value, more important responsibilities. Robotic process automation is one example of basic automation. Robotics is a subgroup of technology in which a robot possesses human-like characteristics. The automated robotic arm is the most humanlike aspect of today's industrial robot. The robot's arm can be programmed to do practical tasks like as loading and unloading items at a manufacturing plant or carrying out a sequence of welding operations.

Process automation automates more complex and repetitive activities that need many phases and interface with a variety of platforms. This type of automation monitors industrial and commercial activities to maintain uniformity and compliance. Automating processes can increase productivity and effectiveness within a business.

It can also offer new perspectives on business and information technology challenges and suggest solutions. Process automation encompasses operations such as process assessment, automated workflows, and handling business processes. Intelligent automation is a very effective form of automation. It combines automated processes, artificial intelligence (AI), and machine learning capabilities. Automated computers can constantly "pick up" and make better decisions based on past experiences and analysis. In the case of client support, virtual advisors driven by AI/ML could reduce costs while empowering customers and human officials, leading to an improved consumer experience.

1.2. Objectives of Automation

Following are the main objectives of automation:

- To reduce manufacturing lead time
- To optimize production activities and processes
- To minimize labour wages
- To enhance machine utilization
- To increase resources utilization
- To maximize inventory utilization
- Timely production
- To improve product quality
- To reduce idle time for machines

1.3. Definition of Automation

"Technology that allows a task to be accomplished without human interaction".

OR

"Automation is the facilitation of processes that do not require human aid to complete".

OR

"The deployment of technology, programming instructions, robotics, or processes that create outcomes with no human involvement".

OR

"Automation is the process of replacing conventional methods of doing work, either with machines or with software programs that make jobs easier that humans have previously handled".

OR

"A program and plan of instructions can be used to successfully implement an automated process".

Basically, industrial automated production process is composed up of an assortment of automated machinery that passes raw materials throughout the process before transforming them into a finished product.

1.3.1. Elements of Automated Process

An automated process consists of the following key elements:

- Power Source
- Plan of Instructions
- Feedback control system

Basic elements of automation process are shown in Fig. 1.1.

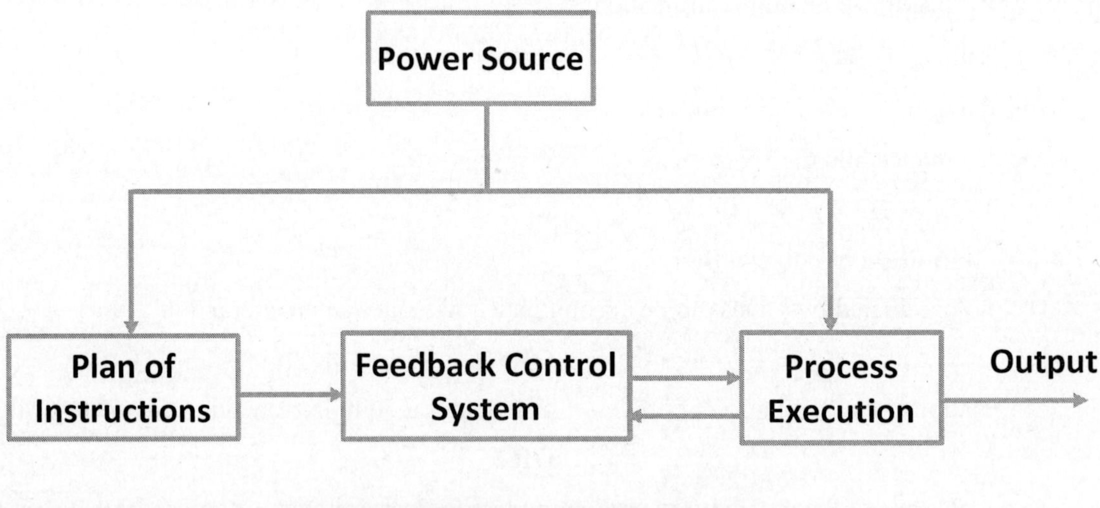

Fig.1.1. Basic elements of automation process

1.3.1.1. Power Source

An automated system is intended to perform a useful function, that requires electricity. Although there are numerous sources of power available, but electricity is the most commonly employed in modern automated systems. Electrical power is the most adaptable as it can be easily created from multiple sources (such as fossil fuels, hydroelectric, solar, wind and nuclear power to carry out important tasks. Furthermore, electrical energy can be retained by efficient, long-lasting batteries.

1.3.1.2. Plan of Instructions

Plan of instructions comprises a programming command connected to feedback control in an automated system in that the program specifies the sequence of values for the inputs of the numerous feedback control loops that make up the automated system.

1.3.1.3. Feedback Control System

In an automated system, the control system is programmed, with a controller that performs the operation automatically. An automated control system preserves or enhances the operation of a controlled equipment. The automated controlled system secondary operations, such as starting, halting, inspection, and changing, are all programmable.

1.4. Benefits of Automation

Automation is often associated with benefits such as increased output and productivity, more efficient material use, higher quality products, increased security, shorter worker workweeks, and shorter production lead times. Higher output and productivity have been two of the most compelling reasons to employ automation. Despite promises of improved quality based on human labor, automated systems frequently complete the manufacturing process with less variability than human workers, resulting in better product control and consistency. Furthermore, increased process control encourages greater material utilization, which leads to less scrap. Worker safety is a primary motivation for automating an industrial operation. Automated systems frequently remove employees from the workplace, shielding them from the hazards of the production environment.

1.5. Drawbacks of Automation

The loss of workers is a significant disadvantage of automation that has been thoroughly investigated. Considering the possible social benefits of retraining displaced individuals for employment elsewhere, almost every worker whose job has been replaced by a machine goes through a period of psychological distress. In addition to being displaced from their employment, the person may be relocated substantially. An individual may need to relocate in order to seek new employment, which increases their stress. The additional drawbacks of automated equipment include the substantial investment in capital required to invest in automation, the need for more maintenance than with a manually regulated machinery, and a typically reduced level of adaptability in terms of product choices as compared to a manually operated system.

1.6. Reasons for Automating

There are many reasons behind automation but the main reasons are:

- Productivity enhancement
- Reduction in labor cost
- To alleviate the implications of labor shortages
- To enhance safety for workers
- To elevate the product's quality and performance
- To minimize the manufacturing delay
- Reliability and accuracy in operations
- Avoid the significant cost of not automating

1.7. Automation Strategies

The following section discusses a few pertinent strategies that are necessary for process automation and simplification:

Specialized Operations

The initial approach is utilizing specialized machinery intended to execute tasks with optimal efficiency. It is a technique that makes use of equipment with specific functions meant to carry out a single task as efficiently as possible. This approach uses specialized labour to manage automation in order to increase productivity.

Combined Operations

A sequence of operations leads to production. It is a method of combining processes on some complicated components in order to reduce the number of standalone manufacturing machines or workstations by which the part must be processed. The primary benefit of this procedure is shorter production lead time.

Synchronous Operations

It is an extension of the combined operation technique that allows for the same operations to be performed continuously in less time. Performing various operating processes on the same work part reduces processing time. It will be beneficial to perform the operations within the allotted time span.

Integration of Processes

It connects multiple workstations into a single integrated process incorporating automated work handling devices. An effective integration and automation framework consists of two key elements: an approach to technology and a framework for operation. The technology plan includes implementing different kinds of automation, integration, and tools and providing services over an integrated platform. The operating model involves establishing procedures for governance and enabling activities so that applications teams and divisions within the company can develop connections and automations independently of one another, but with security and efficiency.

Enhanced Flexibility

It endeavours to maximize the optimum usage of production machinery. By using the same equipment to produce a variety of products. This decreases the time required to properly configure and control machines for production. A simple way to increase flexibility in automation systems is to incorporate adaptive and user-friendly interfaces which enable for real-time alterations. This increases flexibility and accessibility, maintaining therefore the automated system can react immediately to any modifications in the manufacturing system.

Enhanced Material Handling and Retention

It helps to reduce the amount of time spent non-operatively, resulting in a shorter completion time. Automated palletizing, a component of an automated material handling system, considerably eliminates risks associated with the handling of heavy materials. Organizations can improve workplace safety by assigning heavy lifting to automated machinery. The basic function of material handling involves finding safe and cost-effective equipment, selecting production units, and working with plant layout in order to minimize material handling.

Online Assessment

Typically, the process is followed by an assessment for the quality of the work. On-line assessment of the manufacturing process allows modifications to be performed as the product is being produced. This eliminates scrap and improves the overall quantity of product closer to the baseline standards anticipated by the designer.

Process Monitoring and Management

Various control techniques are offered to ensure effective performance of specific procedures and equipment. Process management and monitoring are the methods and strategies used by companies to design, monitor, and govern the procedures they utilize to achieve their goals as efficiently as possible. Process analysts evaluate higher-level or qualitative features of the process.

1.8. Types of Automation

Automation has significantly improved the quality of life for individuals. Automation falls into three categories - fixed, programmable, and flexible as discussed under:

1.8.1. Fixed Automation

Fixed automation is often referred to as strong automation. It is employed when there is a high demand for production and is determined by machine setup. Unlike customized automation, engineers configure fixed automation systems to perform the same action again. The purpose of fixed automation is to develop a collection of automated processes that, when fully integrated, will manufacture a certain product or complete a specific activity from beginning to end. Although fixed automation has a larger initial cost than other options, it pays for itself over time with increased production rates and quantities.

It is perfect for producers who frequently use a variety of manufacturing techniques to produce a single product in massive volumes. All manufacturing operations are integrated into a single, efficient unit through fixed automation. This ensures the quality of the final product while saving time, energy, and labor expenses. Some examples of fixed automation are: automobile industry, material handling unit, operations for assembly, robotic painting etc.

Fixed automation is a cutting-edge and effective manufacturing process in which equipment settings determine the order in which technical activities occur. Fixed automation systems are commonly utilized in production systems that need specialized equipment and huge output volumes. Rigid automation, also known as fixed automated manufacturing, is a system that combines automated assembly and production processes to produce a single product. In this case, the application is usually simple and consists of an assembly or process that is controlled by programmed commands. It might be difficult to accept changes in product design when a fixed automated process is developed for a certain purpose or process per application.

1.8.2. Programmable Automation

Programmable automation is a type of automation employed in batch manufacturing. Automation machines are programmed again and reconfigured multiple times for each lot. Each cycle's programming is written into the structure and executed in an ordered manner. Real-time PLCs, industrial robotic applications, and multipurpose CNC (Computer Numerical Controlled) machine tools are used in programmable automation. Using automation technologies to power machinery and equipment with applied logical programming commands results in operational efficiency.

The design and operation of programmable automation procedures provide manufacturers more manufacturing flexibility. Manufacturing goods in batches allows for personalization. With manufacturing activities guided by a set of instructions, new programs can be created and inserted into the framework in order to conduct every step of manufacturing as required. Programmable variations in the production process allows rapid modifications to products at any time. The equipment used in programmable automation must be designed to be flexible with shifting production requirements. One of the most noteworthy benefits of programmable automation is its adaptability to various operational processes and products configurations.

Manufacturers have a variety of production alternatives because of the capabilities and aesthetics of programmable automation processes. The finished product can be customized due to batch manufacturing. The production processes are managed by a set of instructions, and new programs can be created and added to the system as needed to complete each stage of manufacturing. Programmable changes in the production process allow products to be modified often and at any time.

Programmable automation uses industrial robots and CNC machine equipment. For small to medium volume batch manufacturing of components and parts, the setup is perfect. Physical alterations to the machinery and devices are occasionally needed in addition to programmed changes to the instructions, which can be generated and written in advance to reprogram the system. Machine settings must be changed, and new fixtures and equipment must be installed to make room for the new product. This means that the changeover process, which involves reprogramming and physical setup, needs to be integrated into production.

1.8.3. Flexible Automation

Flexible automation offers more versatility than programmed automation. It facilitates the use of a variety of products or components in batch production while maintaining the optimum amount of time in between. Flexible automation is the ability of a system to quickly and easily perform a task with distinct needs in order to change the product design. Industrial automation technologies increase output and save costs while simplifying operations and procedures in manufacturing plants. Despite the differences between automation technologies, organizations can choose the type of automation system that best fits their needs.

Considering programmable automation can manage a wide range of product types and production volumes, it is the ideal option for organizations that offer small-to-medium-sized production runs. Some examples of flexible automation are: aautomated assembly lines, systems for converting and handling websites, procedures used in the production of chemicals, material conveyor systems, machine transfer lines, Processes for automating paint and coating applications.

The concept of flexible manufacturing emerged all over the 1960s as automated technology was introduced to the production line. This led to the widespread use of robots, programmable controllers, and computer numerical control (CNC) machines on factory floors. Industrial equipment may be trained to do a variety of specialised duties and adapt quickly to these jobs nowadays. This makes organisational procedures more flexible and facilitates seamless transitions between various tasks. Programmable automation brings rise to flexible automation. The time required to reprogrammed and turn out manufacturing machinery for every new batch of product is a disadvantage of programmable automation. This is an expensive example of wasted manufacturing time. The quantity of commodities is sufficiently limited in flexible automation to enable quick and automated equipment changes.

Flexible automation reprogrammes the equipment offline, meaning that it is done at a computer terminal as opposed to the actual manufacturing equipment. This means that different items can be produced in succession rather than having to group similar products into batches. Flexible automation systems often consist of the following:

Machines for Processing Parts: CNC machining equipment handles some of these tasks; additional automated workstations and inspection are used in tandem. System for handling materials: Robots are usually used to load and unload parts from one area of the production line to another using conveyors and other devices.

Centralised Computer Control System: This controller coordinates the operational operations of the machines and provides information on component routing and timing adjustments within the material-handling system through communications.

Human labour: Despite the automation of these systems, engineers are still required to keep an eye on, fix, maintain, and adjust operations as necessary.

1.9. Numerical Control (NC, CNC, DNC)

NC, CNC, and DNC are programming strategies used to automate manufacturing operations. These three titles are frequently used interchangeably; however, they refer to unique machine operation techniques. Numerical control was the first machining technology invented. Then followed the computerized version, Computerized Numerical Control, and the improved version, Direct Numerical Control.

1.9.1. Numerical Control (NC)

Numerical control is a programmable automation system that uses numbers, letters, and symbols to control operations. This command is meant to carry out a specific task. Numerical control machines have the ability to change the programming for each job, which implies that when the job changes, the instructions are updated. Changing program instructions is easier than adapting production equipment. This flexibility reduces overall production costs. Numerical control can quickly respond to design modifications and changes in schedules for production.

Advantages of NC Machine:

The major advantages of Numerical Control Machine are as under:

- Increased industrial productivity
- Numerical control is easily adaptable to engineering design modifications and production schedule shifts
- Flexibility in operation
- Reduced manufacturing lead time
- Reduces floor space requirements

Limitations of NC Machine

Following are the limitations of Numerical Control Machine:

- Conventional NC machines do not provide an option for changing the cutting speed and feed of the operation
- Programming error in punched tape
- Initial investment and maintenance cost is higher
- Required skilled labour
- Wear and tear in punch tape

1.9.2. Computer Numerical Control (CNC)

The term "computer numerical control" refers to a manufacturing process in which the movements of tools and machines are controlled by preprogrammed computer software. These machines, which include lathes, mills, perform processes that were formerly done by hand with accuracy and efficiently. CNC technology can help to enhance manufacturing productivity, accuracy, and flexibility. Computer numerical control (CNC) is a technology that employs computer code to precisely control and automate machine tools such as lathes and milling

machines. CNC machines improve efficiency, accuracy, and reproducibility while decreasing manufacturing time and human error in industrial processes. The widespread use of CNC technology has transformed industries such as aerospace, automotive, and woodworking, enabling the cost-effective production of complicated, high-quality components.

Advantages of CNC

There are several advantages of CNC machine. Some of them are discussed below:

- CNC machines have numerous benefits, including improved precision, speed, and reproducibility.
- They also reduce the human error, increase safety, and allow for the production of complex geometries that would be difficult or impossible to accomplish manually.
- Furthermore, CNC machines can function continuously for 24 hours, which boosts total output. It produces high quality products with minimum wastages.
- Operations of CNC cutting is much higher than manual cutting operations.
- Higher production rate at less production time.

Limitations of CNC

Some of major limitations of CNC machines are listed below:

- Even while CNC machines produce sophisticated forms and designs with exceptional accuracy, their work size capacity is limited.
- The size of the machine's bed or spindle determines the largest workpiece it can hold It's important to know the size constraints of CNC machine while selecting the appropriate equipment for the task.

1.9.3. Direct Numerical Control (DNC)

Direct numerical control machines are advanced numerical control systems that enable several machines to run in real time from a single computer. The direct numerical control system's lack of a tape reader improves machining system reliability. The created part programme is instantly sent from the computer's memory to the machine tool. A single huge computer system can handle over a hundred machines at once. The main computer generates the necessary instructions for each machine on demand. A central computer system is used to store and edit programs for machine tools that are linked to a direct numerical control machine. It combines computer aided design and computer aided manufacturing on a single platform. It also provides a common interface between computers and operators through a network, even if the computers are located far away from the plant. The main components of DNC machines are: computer system (centralized), memory in bulk for program storage, network and numerical control machine.

Advantages of DNC Machine

Some of major advantages are highlighted below:

- Increased adaptability and processing capacity.
- Removal of perforated tapes. One of the primary functions of the Direct Numerical Control machine is to collect data for the purpose of measuring store performance.
- The storage capacity of a direct numerical control system is greater than that of traditional Numerical Control system that store part programmed instructions on tapes.

Limitations of DNC Machine

Following are the limitations of Direct Numerical Control Machine:

- The direct numerical control machine is controlled centrally, and if the computer fails, the entire machine shop's operations stop abruptly.
- DNC is costly and is used in situations where great automation is required.

1.10. Introduction to CNC programming

CNC programming uses three-dimensional product shape and dimension data to generate instructions for a CNC machine that eliminate excess material and form the desired shape. Generally, in order to utilise CAM software for CNC programming, the target part's 3D model must be accessible. CAM software is used by CNC operators to create tool paths based on part geometry, which includes intricate shapes, holes, and slots. After that, the CNC programme, sometimes referred to as G-code, is generated by the CAM software. Next, the CNC machine receives the G-code.

These parameters encompass a wide range of information, such as feed rate, speed, and tool selection. The CNC machine reads and functions on the G-code generated by the CAM software from these toolpath movement instructions and parameters. G codes are geometry-related and regulate the machine motions that generate the part. M codes, which stand for machine or miscellaneous, handle machine movements that do not involve movement, such as turning on or off the spindle. G and M codes activate the CNC machine and its logic controller. M code regulates tool rotation and other operations. The system uses alphanumeric codes beginning with S, T, D, and F to represent characteristics such as speed, tool number, cutter diameter offset, and feed.

When the machine's cycle start button is hit, the steps stated in the code are carried out until the part is completed. The machine control unit loads these instructions into a CNC machine, allowing it to autonomously create a part. CNC machines are now commonly used in industries, replacing earlier manually driven machinery. The reasoning behind this, is to provide more productivity and quality than manual equipment. CNC programming can be performed on a local machine interface using computer-aided manufacturing software.

1.10.1. Types of CNC programming

There are mainly three types:

- Manual CNC programming
- CAM based CNC programming

- Conversational CNC programming

1.10.1.1. Manual CNC programming

The most conventional and time-consuming method is manual CNC programming, which calls for the programmer to predict the machine's responses. This type of programming is suitable for carrying out straightforward operations or creating a particular design.

1.10.1.2. CAM based CNC programming

CAM CNC programming is an excellent approach for those with less experience with complex mathematics. By translating CAD design into the CNC programming language, the software assists in avoiding the majority of the mathematical operations required in the manual programming approach. CAM CNC programming is an excellent approach for those with less experience with complex mathematics. By translating CAD design into the CNC programming language, the software assists in avoiding the majority of the mathematical operations required in the manual programming approach. Several well-known CNC programmes suitable for any level of skill such as Planet CNC, Linux CNC etc.

1.10.1.3. Conversational CNC programming

Beginners can programme a CNC machine with conversational ease because it doesn't require them to understand G-code in order to generate the desired cuts. All the user has to do is enter the relevant information in simple language. In order to maintain the accuracy of the design, this programming language also enables the operator to confirm tool movements prior to programme execution. However, for complicated pathways, this approach is impractical.

1.11. Computer Aided Process Planning

Computer-aided process planning (CAPP) is the utilization of computer technology to assist in the process planning of an item or component in manufacturing. Computer-aided process planning involves creating process route sheets that use either a variant or generative approach. The variant approach typically involves examining standard process plan files and selecting the best option. If the process plan is not suitable, it can be manually modified. The generative approach comprises design algorithms, machine characteristic files, and a decision-making expert system. Expert systems based on decision rules have been used in several generative computer-aided process planning methods. Computer-aided process planning has recently emerged as the most important link between an integrated CAD/CAM system and inter-organizational flow. When grouping of components is required for the operation sequence, an alternative variation strategy is used in computer-aided process planning known as retrieval computer aided process planning.

1.11.1. Need of Computer Aided Process Planning

- To identify how the part, manufacturing, quality, and cost connect.
- Effectively develop a precise and reliable process plan.
- Minimise the expenditure and lead time for process planning.
- Less expertise is needed for process planners.
- Enhanced efficiency of the process planner
- Simple interface for further investigation with other application programs

1.11.2. Types of Computer Aided Process Planning (CAPP)

It includes generative, variant, and retrieval process planning. Generative CAPP is typically used to develop a new plan for adding a new part automatically and without the need for human intervention, whereas variant CAPP is commonly used when the new part requires change. Retrieval CAPP is a form of CAPP in which sections are grouped together based on their similarity in operations and sequencing. The types of computer-aided process planning are explored in detail below.

Generative CAPP

Generative computer assisted process planning refers to a method for automatically creating a process plan that contains a new component. It automatically synthesises process information to generate a process plan for a new component without requiring human participation. Generative CAPP focuses on the framework and benefits of computer-aided process planning in great depth. No existing plans are included in this framework. It can generate process plans for both new and existing components or parts. Process plans are created using decision logic, formulas, technological algorithms, geometry-based data, a geometry-based coding scheme, and process information in the form of decision logic and data to make unique judgements for transforming raw materials to a finished product.

Variant CAPP

A process plan for a new part is developed by recalled, recognizing, and acquiring a prior strategy for a similar part, and then implementing the requisite changes for the new part. The main focus of variant computer aided process planning is to make a process plan for a new part is developed by recalled, recognizing, and acquiring a prior strategy for a similar part, and then implementing the requisite changes for the new part. It includes, define the coding scheme, divide the parts into part families and create a standardised process strategy, retrieve and edit the current plan.

Retrieval CAPP

The foundation of retrieval CAPP is group technology. It is also known by variant computer aided process planning. Group technology is the idea of organising components according to how similarly their operation sequences or geometrical features are. As a database, experts' knowledge and standard operating procedures according to group technology are required. There is a lot of work involved in organising and collecting data. It is simple to use, learn, and construct. The process plan still needs to be edited by experienced process planners. Without additional process planning, it cannot be used in a fully automated manufacturing system.

Unit Summary

This chapter covers the basics of automation, its various types, including architecture, addressing modes, and instruction sets, CNC programming, and the fundamentals of computer-aided process planning. It also explores the various computer-aided processes that use computer technology to help with the process planning of an item or component in production.

Solved Examples

1. Why is it crucial to comprehend the definition of a test automation framework?

Ans1. A test automation framework is an assemblage of guidelines, instruments, and procedures designed to streamline and enhance the automated testing procedure. It is important because it creates a uniform methodology, which reduces maintenance expenses and boosts test effectiveness. Automation frameworks facilitate the integration of many technologies, scalability, and reuse of code. They guarantee testing uniformity, which improves its dependability and comprehension. Incorporating a test automation framework enhances the software development lifecycle's overall quality significantly.

2. What sets automated testing apart from manual testing, and how does it work?

Ans2. While manual testing necessitates human engagement during the same process, automation testing uses specialist software tools to execute a test case suite. Automated testing saves time and guarantees consistency by running tests automatically. Although manual testing is slower and more prone to human mistake, it yields more intuitive insights. In contrast to manual testing, automation testing enables tests to run on a variety of platforms and devices

for 24 hours a day, seven days a week. Automation testing involves technical skills and can be more expensive to set up initially than manual testing.

3. What benefits do automated testing provide over conventional testing?

Ans3. Compared with conventional testing, automation testing offers a number of benefits, such as enhanced precision, recurrence and dependability. Automation testing allows for faster feedback cycles by significantly reducing the amount of time required for recurrent test execution. Complex test cases that are challenging to complete manually can be executed with this kind of testing. Test coverage is increased with automation testing, which also facilitates performance, load, and stress testing. Moreover, comprehensive logs produced by automated testing facilitate fault monitoring.

4. Describe the idea of automated keyword-driven testing.

Ans4. Automated testing that uses keywords to indicate particular activities or tests that will be run on the application under test is known as keyword-driven testing. By separating test data from test automation logic, this method enables non-technical stakeholders to participate in test design. Keywords simplify complicated test scripts into simple, readable sentences. Test cases become more reusable, maintenance is made easier, and the variety of the test automation suite is increased using keyword-driven testing. It is possible to build and run tests efficiently with this methodology.

5. Describe the test data management procedure for automated testing.

Ans5. When managing test data for automated testing, make use of a centralised test data management system. Automation testers generate, manage, and maintain data sets in a common database to ensure consistency and accessibility. Using external data sources like files and databases enables the production and modification of dynamic data. Automation frameworks that incorporate several data sources enable testing in a variety of realistic data scenarios. Automation testers must routinely clean and update test information to accommodate real-world events in order to improve test dependability and correctness.

6.) Which automated testing issues are most common, and how can they be resolved?

Ans6. Maintaining test data, guaranteeing script reusability, and handling dynamic elements are prevalent issues in automated testing. A robust framework architecture incorporating dynamic locator methods for web element updates is important to overcome these issues. Using data-driven approaches and modularizing test scripts are necessary to increase script reusability. Using centralised data repositories and external data sources, automation testers efficiently handle test data. These problems are reduced by routine framework evaluations and changes, which leads to effective and successful automation testing.

Exercises

1. What do you mean by automation Process? Write down its elements.
2. Define briefly various types of automation strategies?
3. What do you mean by variant CAPP? How it is different from generative CAPP?
4. Introduce CNC and its types?
5. Differentiate between CNC and DNC.
6. How CNC programming works?
7. Write down advantages and limitations of NC, CNC and DNC.
8. What is a need of automation in industries?

Multiple Choice Questions

1. Automation systems are also called:
   a. Process automation
   b. Automatic technique
   c. Manual process
   d. None of these

2. Which of the following statements are true about the automation process?
   a. It is a method that automatically manages processes, such as pulp factories
   b. It is a method that uses robots to control processes, such as those in pulp industries

c. It is a procedure that controls processes, such as pulp factories that use humans

d. None of the preceding

3. An automation system is associated with:

   a. System of distributed control

   b. Data collection and supervisory control system

   c. Unique control mechanism

   d. Both a and b

4. DCS represents:

   a. Distributed control system

   b. Disturbed control server

   c. Digital control system

   d. None of these

5. The process automation system has a ______ level of automation.

   a. High level

   b. Equal

   c. Low Level

   d. None of the above

6. The following operations are not performed in CNC machining centres:

   a. Milling

   b. Boring

   c. Welding

   d. Tapping

7. Multiple microprocessors and programmable logic controllers' function in CNC systems.

   a. Consecutively

   b. In series

   c. In parallel

   d. For 80% of the overall machining time

9. How many classifications are there for CNC machine tool systems?

   a. 2

   b. 3

c. 4

d. 5

10. CNC machining requires qualified part programmers.

a. True

b. False

11. Which of the following constitutes automation control?

a. Programmable Logic Controller

b. Electronic controller with logic gates

c. Hardwired logic controller

d. All of the aforementioned

12. What is the aim of specialized workstations?

a. More users with a lower computer workload

b. High cost

c. Lower efficiency

d. All of the aforementioned

13. Which of the following describes automation's advantages?

a. Extended lead time for manufacturing

b. Limited capital investment

c. No labour force required

d. Enhanced safety for workers

14. Automation is not suitable in case of _________

a. Labour shortages

b. Improving product quality

c. Short product life cycle

d. Reducing manufacturing lead time

15. Which is not one of the 10 automation and process improvement strategies?

a. Multi-tasking

b. Operational specialization

c. Manual processes

d. Online inspections

16. In DCS production, how many levels are there?

a. Three

b. Four

c. Five

d. Six

Answers for multiple choice questions:

Keys for multiple choice questions: 1(a), 2(a), 3(d), 4(c), 5(c), 6(c), 7(c), 8(a), 9(d), 10(a), 11(d), 12(a), 13(d), 14(a), 15(c), 16(b)

KNOW MORE

For more information related to this topic scan the QR code,

OR

Type this link in your browser

https://ufile.io/im605s8j

References

1. Prof. Siddhartha Mukhopadhyay, NEPTEL course, Industrial Automation and Control, https://onlinecourses.nptel.ac.in/noc21_me67/preview

2. Mikell P. Groover, Automation, Production Systems and Computer Integrated Manufacturing, Fourth Edition, Pearson. USA (2015)

3. https://www.pega.com/process-automation

4. https://www.conceptmachines.net/

5. https://cdn.automationdirect.com/static/eBooks/Control-System-Engineering-eBook.pdf

2 MACHINE AND PROCESS AUTOMATION

UNIT SPECIFICS

This chapter provides an in-depth exploration of machine and process automation, which is required for effective automated systems. Furthermore, it discusses about and emphasizes the importance of different CNC machines used in industries.

RATIONALE

Machine and process automation are regarded as essential components in the automation industry. If one needs to know these specifics in detail, then understanding of it will be helpful.

PRE-REQUISITE

Knowledge of CNC Machine

UNIT OUTCOMES

List of outcomes of this unit is as follows:

U2-O1: Students should be able to understand the CNC machines and its types.

U2-O2: Students should be able to know about Automated flow lines (types, selection)

U2-O3: Students should be able to understand work part transfer and transfer mechanism and adaptive machine controls overview

Unit Outcomes	Expected Mapping with Programme Outcomes *(1- Weak Correlation; 2- Medium correlation; 3- Strong Correlation)*					
	PO-1	PO-2	PO-3	PO-4	PO-5	PO-6
U2-O1	3	1	3	1	1	2
U2-O2	3	3	2	2	2	3
U2-O3	3	3	1	2	1	3

This chapter provides an overview of the basic industrial framework, as well as the varieties of CNC machines and automated flow lines. The evolution and developments of automated flow lines are covered in this chapter. More details about work part transport and transfer mechanisms, as well as the advantages of feedback systems and control, are provided to readers. The overview of CNC, automated flow lines, methods for work part transport and transfer, feedback systems, and control in this chapter Its main component consists of reconfigurable and modular machinery. The unit concludes with a discussion of adaptive machine controls. The overview of the positive and negative feedback systems in the feedback control system is provided in this work.

2. CNC Machines

2.1. Introduction

A CNC machine is a numerically controlled machine equipped with an inbuilt computer. The onboard computer functions as an equipment control unit, performing a variety of processes. Numerical control machines often include intrinsic control panels that manage all machine activities through the controller's hardware. The CNC machine is equipped with a software-based computer that is pre-programmed with machine operations that remain active even after the machine turns off. The computer memory that holds such information is known as read-only memory (ROM). The machine control unit is in charge of allowing data entry for the execution of each program. Such programs are kept in RAM, but are lost once the CNC machine is turned off. The machine control unit is responsible for facilitating data entering for each program's execution. These programs are kept in RAM, but are lost when the CNC machine is turned off.

These programs can be saved on a variety of media, including punched tape, magnetic tape, and magnetic discs. In the latest version of CNC, machine control units have graphical interfaces that display the CNC programming, cutter routes, and challenges. CNC machining is a traditional subtractive manufacturing method in which layers of material are removed from a standard product using machine tools and computerized controls to produce a bespoke result. CNC stands for "computer numerical control." This approach can be used to treat a wide range of materials, including metals, polymer compounds, glass, glassware, wood, foam, and composite materials. It is employed in a variety of sectors, including big CNC machining, CNC machining telecom component parts, and CNC machining aerospace components, which demand tighter tolerances than other industries.

In contrast to fundamental or additive manufacturing, which includes techniques like liquid injection moulding or 3D printers, subtractive manufacturing techniques like CNC machining are commonly demonstrated. While additive processes incorporate layers of material together to develop the required form and constructive operations distort and shift the stock material to acquire the desired shape, subtractive procedures eliminate layers of materials from the object being worked on to create unique forms and designs.

The controlled nature of CNC machining permits the fabrication of simple parts, with excellent accuracy and precision, and cost-effectiveness during one-time and medium-volume manufacturing processes. Even though CNC machining has certain benefits over conventional manufacturing processes, there are limits to the degree of part design intricacy and complexity that can be reached, as well as the cost of producing intricate parts. While there are benefits and drawbacks to any production method, this article focuses on CNC machining, outlining the basic steps involved as well as the various parts and tools of the CNC machine.

2.2. Objectives of CNC

The major objectives of CNC are discussed below:

To Increase Accuracy Level

Machining centers achieve perfection that conventional hand-operated machines cannot match. Machining centers require high accuracy to execute work within restricted tolerances. The machine executes a set of instructions using a computer program, eliminating any errors created by the machine's operator. This produces considerably less waste because fewer parts are eliminated.

To Enhance Efficiency

The CNC machine is capable of repeating the same task for several hours, saving a lot of time. Since the machines are controlled by computerized designs, there is no need for preliminary drawings. Machining centers in a typical manufacturing setup will continue to operate continuously for days after the work plan with all relevant parameters has been entered into the CNC computer.

Flexibility in Operations

CNC machines are flexible, with applications in the aviation, automotive, and plastics industries, as well as for medical device manufacturing. Their versatility originates from their capacity to construct a wide range of objects from various materials. Although the choice of a CNC machine is primarily determined by the type of item, shape and size, and structure, as well as the desired level of precision, allowing them to quickly respond to the degree of complexity of parts that need to be created.

Optimized Lean Manufacturing

Lean manufacturing is an organization strategy that emphasizes focused resources strictly on delivering benefits for consumers through offering high-quality goods on time, economically, effectively, and with maximum efficiency, while avoiding operations that fail to accomplish this objective. The machining center's aim is to improve lean manufacturing by significantly lowering process cycle time and increasing adaptability, resulting in enhanced final product quality. CNC machines are designed to perform many operations rapidly, accurately, and efficiently, thus enhancing productivity.

2.3. Components of CNC machines

Main components of CNC machines are input device, machine control unit, tools unit, driving unit, feedback unit, display unit as shown in Fig. 2.1.

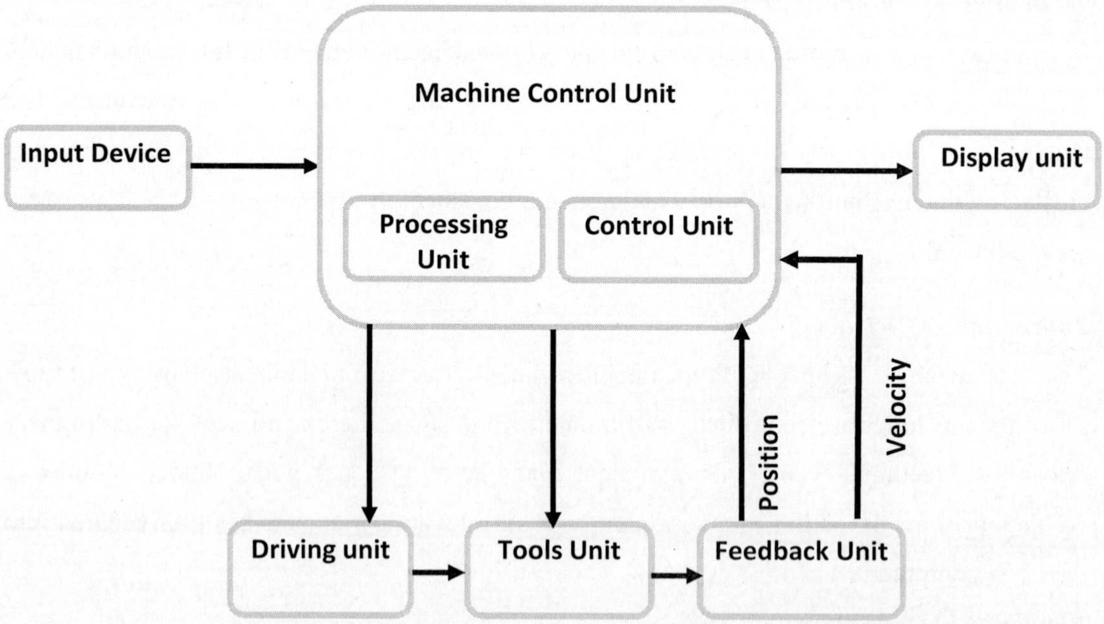

Fig. 2.1. Schematic diagram of a CNC machine

Input Device

These are the devices used to program parts in a CNC machine. Computers, punch tape readers, and magnetic tape readers are three major input devices.

Machine Control Unit

It comprises a set-up of processing and control units that are responsible for the selection of tasks and are referred to as the heart of the CNC machine. It controls the axis mechanism, picks tools according to operations, reads and decodes coding instructions, sets up motion commands, and manages auxiliary control functions such as coolant, spindle on/off, and tool changing. It provides position and velocity information. Simply stated, it handles all aspects of CNC machine control.

Driving unit

A CNC machine's driving unit consists of amplification circuits, drives, and ball screws. The machine control unit provides position and speed signals for each axis to amplifier circuits. The control signals are then amplified to power the driving motors. The actuating drive motors rotate the ball lead screw to position the machine table.

Tools unit

To control its position and velocity, a CNC machine tool must have a slide table and a spindle. The X and Y axis control the machine's work surface, and the Z axis controls the spindle.

Feedback Unit

The feedback system includes transducers that function as sensors. It is also known as a measurement system. It consists of position and speed transducers that continuously monitor the cutting tool's position and speed at any given time. The machine control unit takes inputs from transducers and uses the difference between reference and feedback signals in order to create control signals that alleviate position and speed issues.

Display unit

The monitor displays the CNC machine's programs, commands, and other essential data. It is important because the displayed data will be used to execute the operation.

2.4. Types of CNC Machines

Following are the types of CNC Machines:

- CNC Milling Machine
- CNC Plasma Cutting
- CNC Laser Cutting
- CNC Electric Discharge Machine (EDM)
- CNC Lathe Machine
- 5-Axis CNC Machine
- CNC Router
- Pick and Place CNC Machine

2.4.1. *CNC Milling Machine*

The majority of milling machine configurations include three to six axis. A multi-point milling cutter is used in this machine to assist machine the components. This tool is used to create slots, bores, and holes in the workpiece. Spur gears can also be made with it. In reference to the CNC milling machine, the software is programmed into the memory of the device using G and M codes. It is capable of carrying out its duties in accordance with the work distribution across the coordinates in the program. When compared to traditional milling machines, the CNC milling machine has a very high level of efficiency. The schematic view of CNC milling machine is shown in Fig. 2.2.

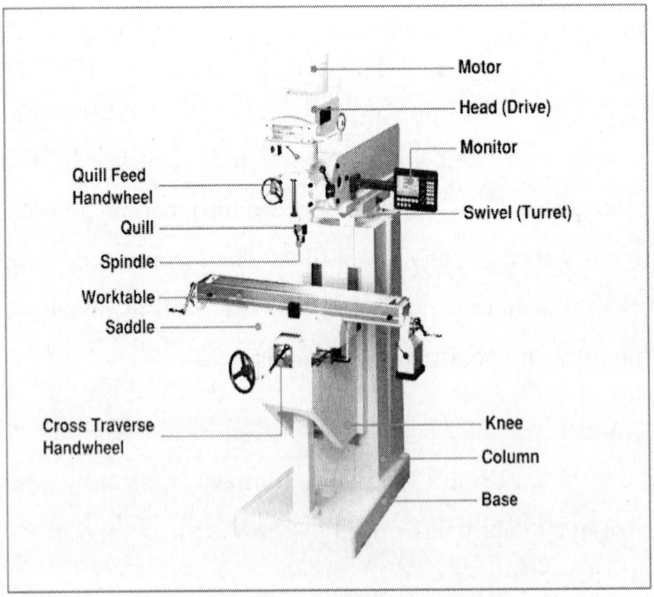

Fig. 2.2. CNC Milling Machine

2.4.2. CNC Plasma Cutting

Plasma cutting CNC, which operate in exactly the same manner as CNC laser cutting machines, are used to cut the materials. Rather than using laser cutting technology, a plasma flame is being used to cut even harder materials. The plasma has a temperature greater than 20,000 degrees Celsius. CNC plasma cutting machine is illustrated in Fig. 2.3.

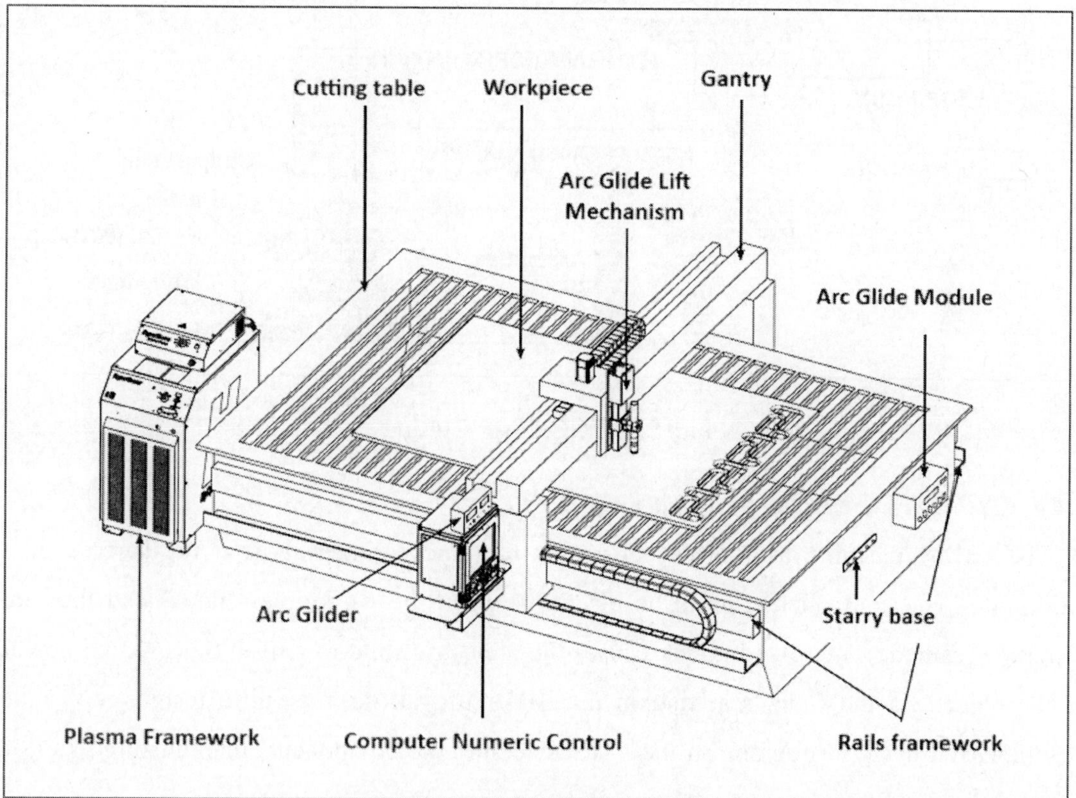

Fig. 2.3. CNC Plasma Cutting

2.4.3. CNC Laser Cutting

The efficiency is quite excellent when compared to hand laser cutting. It is commonly used to cut metal sheets. These are intended to cut tougher materials and are similar to plasma cutting, which uses a plasma torch instead of a laser flame to cut the materials. Laser Cutting CNC machines uses three types of lasers. They are neodymium (Nd), carbon dioxide (CO_2), or yttrium aluminium garnet. The detailed view of CNC Laser Cutting machine is shown in Fig. 2.4.

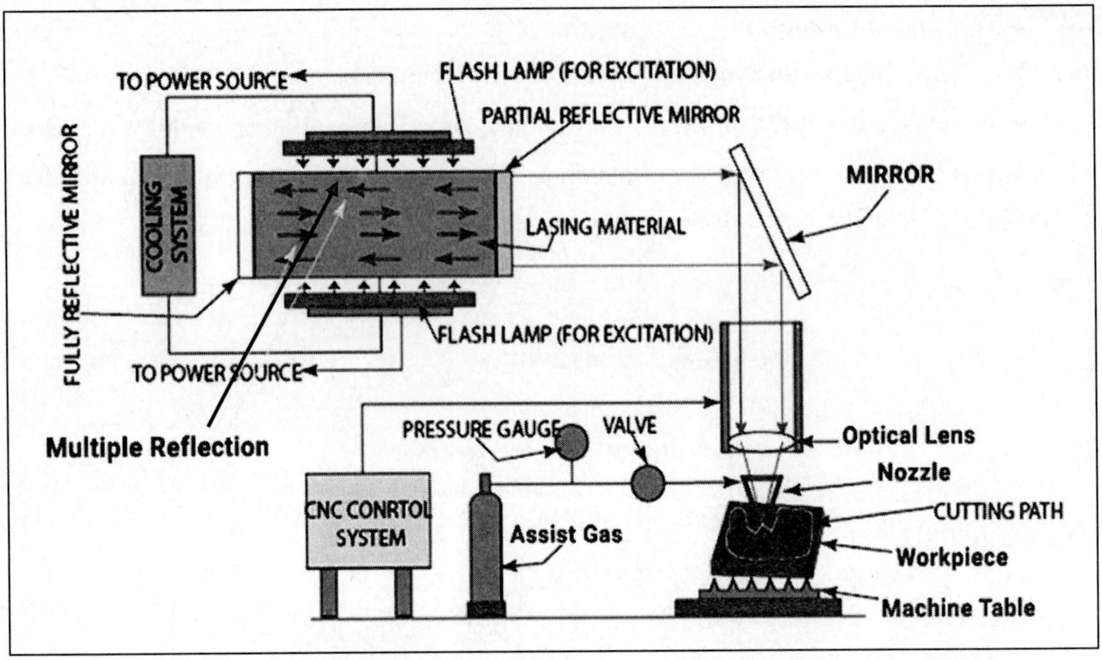

Fig. 2.4. CNC Laser Cutting

2.4.4. CNC Electric Discharge Machine (EDM)

A CNC EDM machine uses electrical sparks to remove material from the surface of a workpiece. The component should be placed between the worktable (anode) and the tool electrode (cathode). Increased power causes the dielectric fluid to ionise, transmitting power to the object via the fluid, resulting in material removal. As the entire technique can be accomplished using a program on the CNC machine, the components manufactured have a better surface finish than traditional machines.

Electrical Discharge, CNC These devices, also referred to as EDM machines, are employed to eliminate material from an object and achieve standards that are not achievable with conventional machining techniques. Electrical spark erosion (EDM) is a non-contact manufacturing technology that removes materials from a workpiece. Objects that are

impractical to build using other methods can be made with EDM. Since EDM doesn't apply cutting forces to the workpiece, it's perfect for operations that require more sensitivity. Double head CNC EDM Machine is shown in Fig. 2.5.

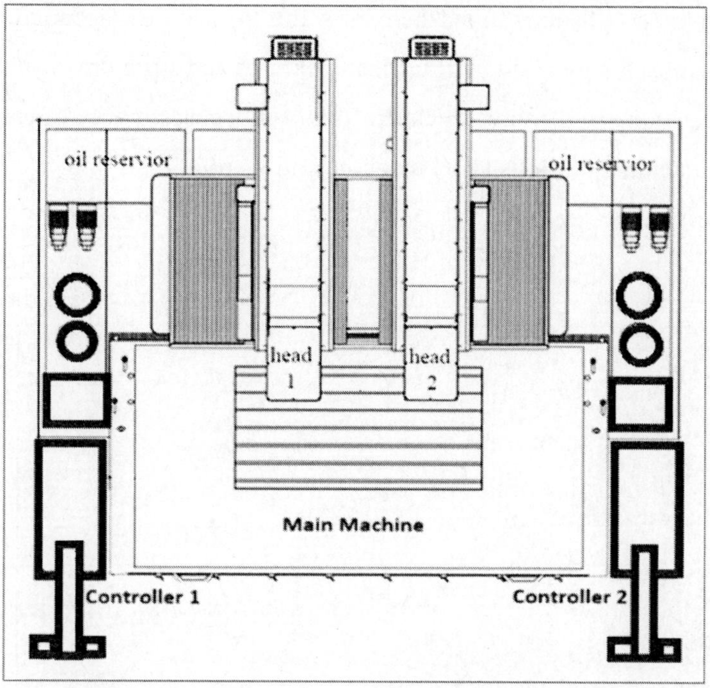

Fig. 2.5. Double head CNC EDM Machine

2.4.5. 5-Axis CNC Machine

Over the past few years, CNC machining equipment has moved from elementary machine tools to greater sophisticated technologies. Currently, one of the most sophisticated techniques accessible is 5-axis CNC machining. With the use of subtractive machining technology, it provides countless options for producing parts. This method entails utilizing five-axis cutting tools to shape and size workpieces into the desired shapes and sizes. The accuracy, precision, efficiency, and dependability of 5-axis machining are all increased.

5-axis milling machines perform better than their competitors' equipment because they have more axis. Moreover, computer numerical control is supported for complete automation and management of the process. In order to deliver accurate CNC machining services, a large number of respectable CNC machine shops rely on this technology. Cutting tools are moved simultaneously along five axis during this procedure.

Five-axis CNC machines combine two rotating and three linear axis to manufacture intricate parts. This often gives the worktable or tool spindles considerable inclined, enabling more rotation and movement. Machine operators can create up to five faces in a single operation with the addition of a fifth axis. This increases the procedure's accuracy and efficiency. Furthermore, it enables the production of intricate features and structures with little setup. This process is growing more and more crucial in many industries since different objects need precise five-face machining. 5-axis CNC machine and its rotation is shown in Fig. 2.6 (a) and Fig. 2.6 (b) respectively.

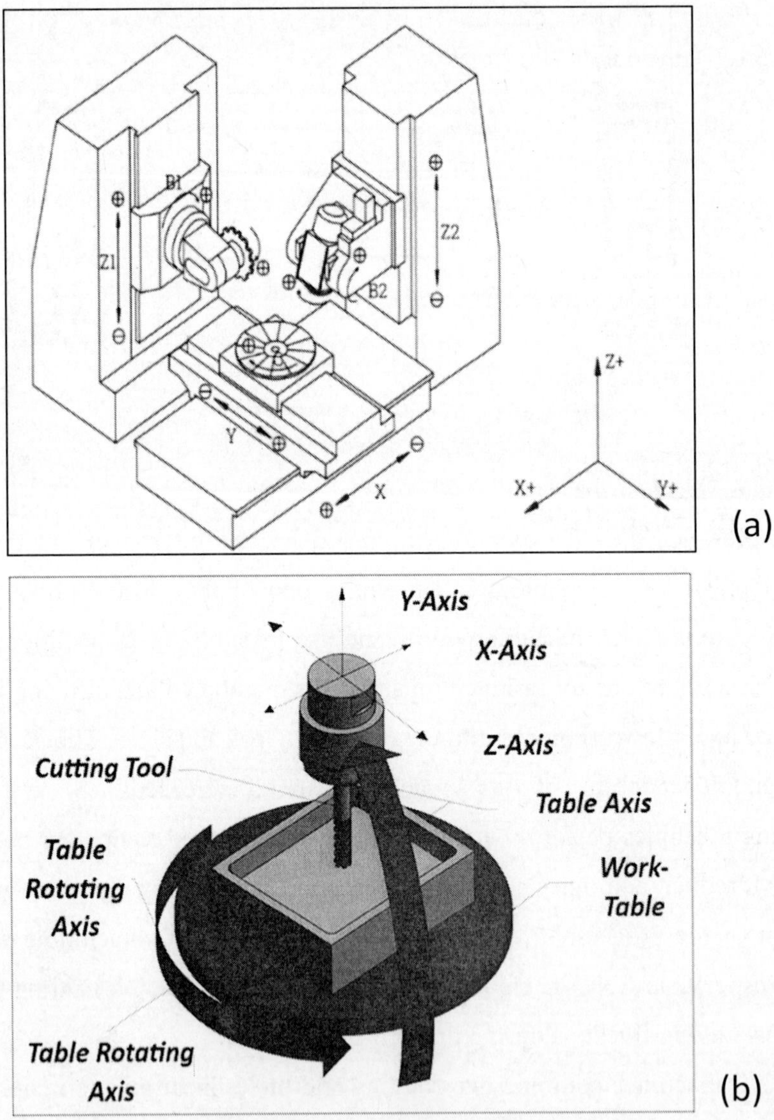

Fig. 2.6. (a) 5-Axis CNC Machine (b) 5-Axis Rotation

2.4.6. CNC Router

A CNC router uses a rotary tool to remove material from soft metals, wooden, plastic, and stretched foam made of polyurethane. This process is known as subtractive manufacturing. When a CNC router is built in a gantry configuration, its spindle travels left and right along the x-axis and back and forth on the y axis. A CNC router differs from a normal CNC mill in that it is not intended for high-speed cutting of complex designs in hard metals. Gantry-style CNC routers are less robust than normal CNC mills, especially when cutting harder metals. As a result, they are limited to cutting softer materials such as wood, mild metals, and occasionally steel. It's also important to note that routers have limited z-axis motion. The schematic view of CNC router is shown in Fig. 2.7.

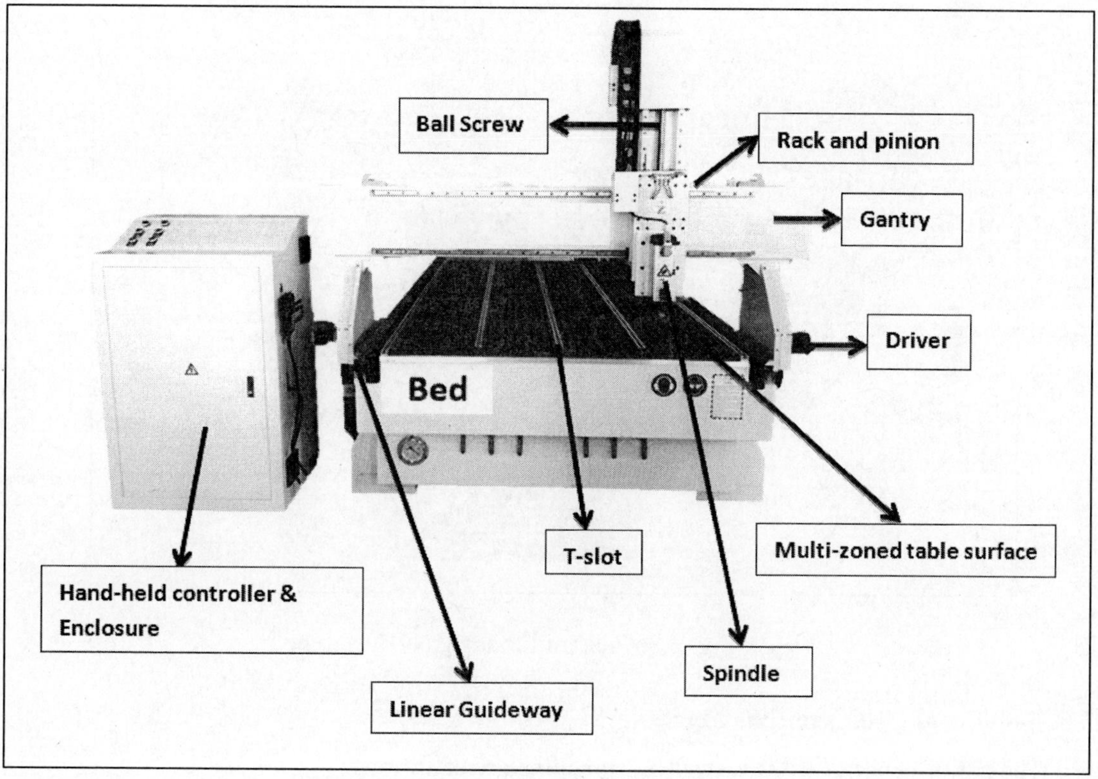

Fig. 2.7. CNC Router

Pick and Place CNC Machine

Pick and Place Automated tools for manufacturing, or CNC machines, carry components and raw materials across a work area. It is employed in the production of many different goods and parts, including as consumer electronics and medical equipment. This device precisely picks up, moves, and dumps things in predetermined areas using computer-controlled robotics. When mass producing things, the extremely precise movements provide the manufacturer more control over the process, saving both time and money. Over the years, this technology has proven to be incredibly effective at raising output at a low cost while maintaining quality requirements. The schematic representation of pick and place CNC machine is shown in Fig. 2.8.

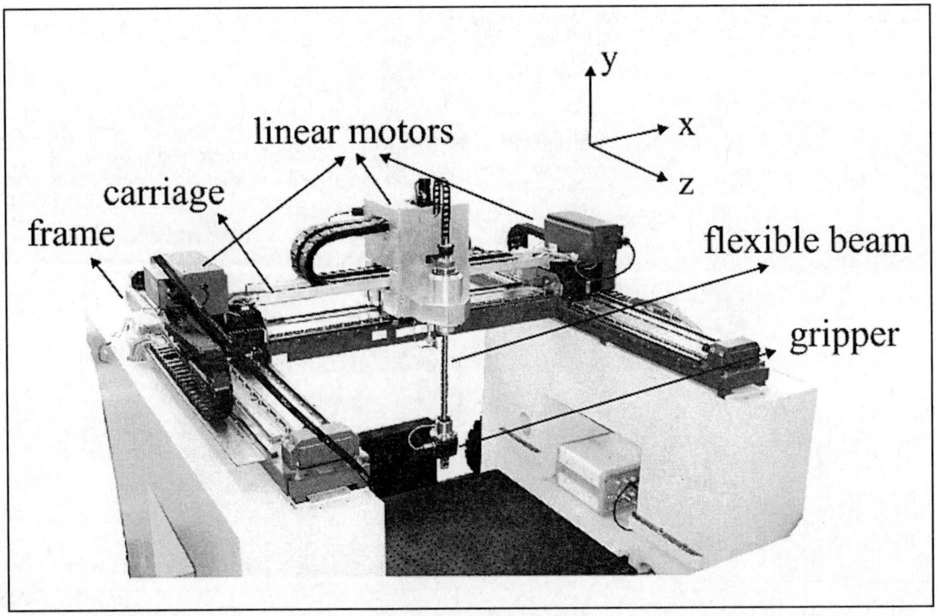

Fig. 2.8. Pick and Place CNC Machine

2.5. Benefits of CNC over NC Machine

The major benefits of CNC over NC machine are as follows:

- A reduction in the number of components required to add a machine operation. Additional features can be programmed into the machine control unit using programming

- A CNC program can be stored or executed directly at the computer numerical control machine.
- Multiple CNC programs can be stored in machine control unit.

2.6. Automated flow lines

An automated flow line integrates multiple machinery or workstation by utilizing work handling devices to transport parts among workstations. Workstations autonomously transport parts and execute specialists' tasks. An automated flow line consists of several machines or workstations which are linked together by work handling devices that transfer parts between

the stations. The transfer of work parts occurs automatically and the workstations carry out their specialized functions automatically. Flow line automation aims to minimize labour costs, enhance production rates, eliminate work-in-process, reduce intervals between activities, specialize processes, and integrate them.

Different types of configurations used in automated flow line process are listed below:

2.6.1. Inline Configuration

2.6.2. Rotary Configuration

2.6.1. Inline Configuration

In line configuration is widely used in industries where layouts are more spacious and on the basis of layouts machines are arranged in continuous or segmented form. The main objective of this type of configuration is to improve productivity and reduce complexity in work parts transfer process from one workstation to another. Inline configuration can be further divided into two categories:

2.6.1.1. Straight In-line Configuration

In-line configurations consist of workstations (W/S) arranged in a straight line, as illustrated in the schematic diagram of straight in-line configuration. An example of a straight in-line transfer machine for machining operations is shown in Fig. 2.9.

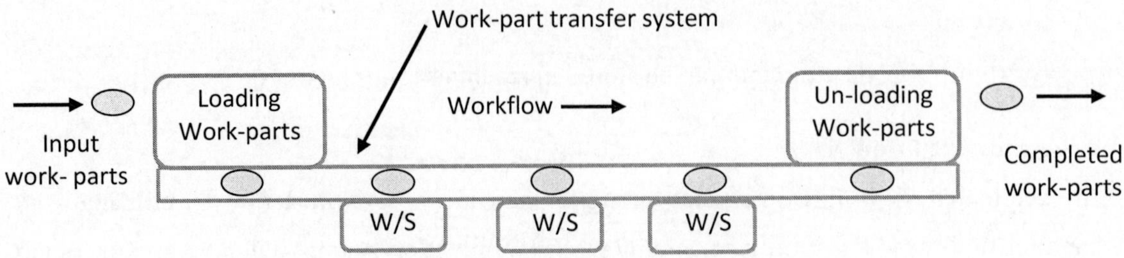

Fig. 2.9. Straight In-line Configuration

2.6.1.2. Segmented Inline Configuration

As seen in the figure 2.10. the segmented in-line configuration is composed up of workstations are arranged in two or more straight lines which are perpendicular to one another and may include an L, U, or rectangular shape. Straight-line arrangements may have a few right-angle twists due to workpiece reorientation, plant layout restrictions, or other causes. These arrangements may be in other orientations depending on industrial needs.

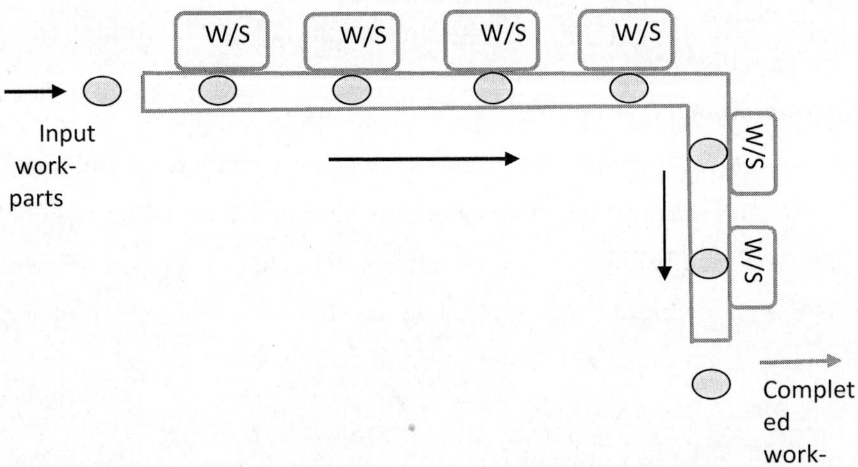

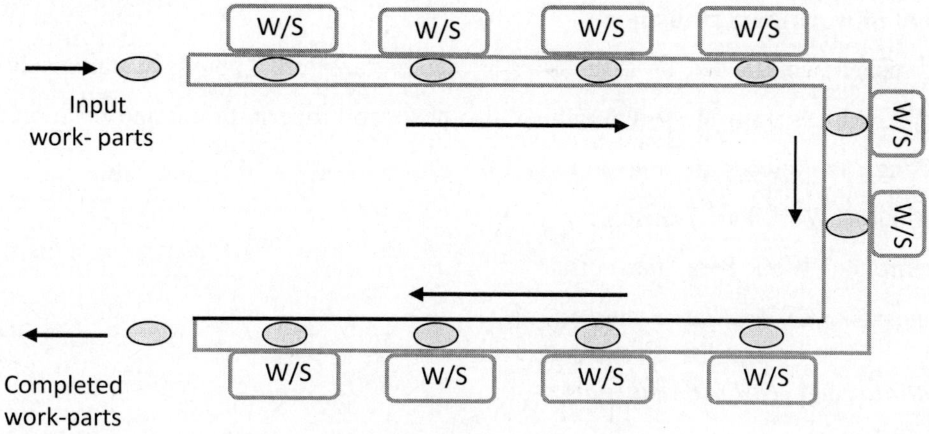

where W/S = workstation

Fig. 2.10. Segmented In-line Configuration

2.6.2. Rotary configuration

The rotating design indexes workpieces on a circular platform. Stationary workstations often appear at the dial's outer boundaries. The revolving table allocates parts to different stations for processing or assembly. This type of equipment, known as a dial indexing machine. This setup is quite usual because it takes up less space and has a faster work-part transfer rate due to the dial indexing configuration. Because of the short travel distance, work-part transfer is remarkably fast in the rotary design as illustrated in Fig. 2.11.

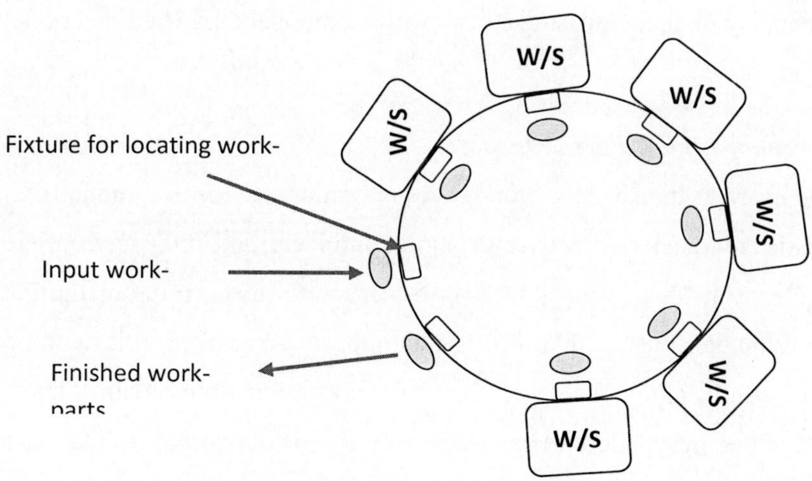

Fig. 2.11. Rotary Configuration

where W/S = workstation

2.7. Method of work-part transport

Partially finished workpieces or assemblies must be transferred between stations by the automated flow line's transfer system, which also needs to properly orient and position them for processing. Workpieces are transported on flow lines in three different ways:

- Continuous Work-Part Transport
- Synchronous Work-Part Transport
- Asynchronous Work-Part Transport

2.7.1. Continuous Work-Part Transport

The continuous approach indicates that workpieces will be transported on a consistent basis. Work-heads must move throughout the operation in order to maintain a consistent identification with the workpiece. The work head cannot move while processing is in progress for a variety of reasons. Transfer lines may not be cut using this process due to inertial difficulties induced by the work heads' weight and size.

In some circumstances, continuous transfer is quite practical. Continuous transfer systems are straightforward to design and manufacture, allowing for high rates of production. Continuous transfer is the movement of workpieces along an automated conveyor or transfer system. This process is basic and effective. It is ideal for lightweight materials that require manual handling. The conveyor system may be continuous from beginning to end or segmented if the flow line is long. Depending on the requirements, the work component may be fixed or detachable from the conveyors.

2.7.2. Synchronous Work-Part Transport

This method involves transporting workpieces intermittently or discontinuously. Workstations are fixed, parts are transferred between stations, and identified at the appropriate locations for execution. The term "synchronous work-part transport" refers to the method of transporting work-parts simultaneously. During synchronous transfer, work components move synchronously and continuously to the next workstation downstream. This technology is widely used in automated flow lines. Workstations conduct specialized tasks, and automatic work part transfers occur instantaneously. Operators never run out of work since the next unit arrives on time.

2.7.3. Asynchronous Work-Part Transport

The asynchronous transfer mechanism allows each work part to proceed to the next station once the current station's processing is complete. Each part rotates independently of the others. As a result, certain parts go through processing on the production line while others are transferred between stations. Asynchronous transfer mechanisms provide more flexibility than the other two techniques, which can be advantageous in some situations.

Asynchronous systems can easily provide in-process storage of work parts. This type of system may solve line balance issues, including considerable changes in processing times between stations. Prolonged operations may require parallel or series stations, whereas shorter procedures may utilise a single station. Thus, average production rates can be substantially equated. Asynchronous lines are frequently used for manually controlled stations where cycle-time changes may cause problems in continuous or synchronous transport systems. Asynchronous systems can accommodate larger workpieces. The disadvantage of this system is its slower cycle rate compared to other systems.

2.8. Transfer Mechanism

Various transfer mechanisms are used to move parts between stations. There are two types of mechanisms that are generally used:

1. Linear Transfer Mechanism
2. Rotary Transfer Mechanism

2.8.1. Linear Transfer Mechanism

Precision conveyors and linear transfer units are the two most prevalent linear transfer systems utilised in manufacturing automation. Linear Transfer Units can precisely transfer a moving object over short or long distances, making them ideal for transporting robots, tool containers, and other types of automation applications. Precision conveyors have numerous applications, including assembly and container filling.

A linear transfer unit is a mechanism that transports automated machinery, components, or parts across a manufacturing line. They improve automated production capabilities by introducing a new axis to operate on. Using a forklift to handle palletized components lowers the requirement for human intervention. They have a variety of applications, including the

Robot Transfer Unit, which guides a 6-axis robot across a production line by linking it to a track and cart called the Linear Transfer Unit. Other uses include tool delivery, collecting, and bin/bowl feeding. A Linear Transfer Unit may perform any job previously assigned to a robot or manufacturing unit.

Precision conveyors are another type of linear transfer system. They are intended to be an essential element of a linear production process that requires precision, velocity, and quality. Because they are designed to be stand-alone links, there are numerous ways in which they can be connected to parts and components. Each link is joined to the next to form a continuous run, which is usually a straight line with looping curves at both ends. The most common understanding of them is as completely linear systems, even though they can be curved. Each link's cam follower makes sure the system stays inside the boundaries of the uniquely made rails. Each joint in the system has specialized needle bearings to minimize wear failure and increase system longevity because of the system's potential for significant weight.

2.8.2. Rotary Transfer Mechanism

One kind of machine tool that can produce a lot of parts quickly is the rotary transfer machine. The machine consists of a sizable indexing table with machining workstations all around it. Geneva mechanisms, ratchet and pawl systems, and rack and pinion systems are examples of frequently used rotational transfer systems.

2.8.2.1. Rack and Pinion

Despite its simplicity, this mechanism is considered to be inappropriate for the high-speed operation that usually occurs in indexing devices. The mechanism for turning the pinion gear and the indexing table that goes with it are shown in the image below. The rack is propelled by a piston. Rotation can occur in the preferred direction with the use of a clutch or similar device. Rack and pinion mechanism is shown in Fig. 2.12.

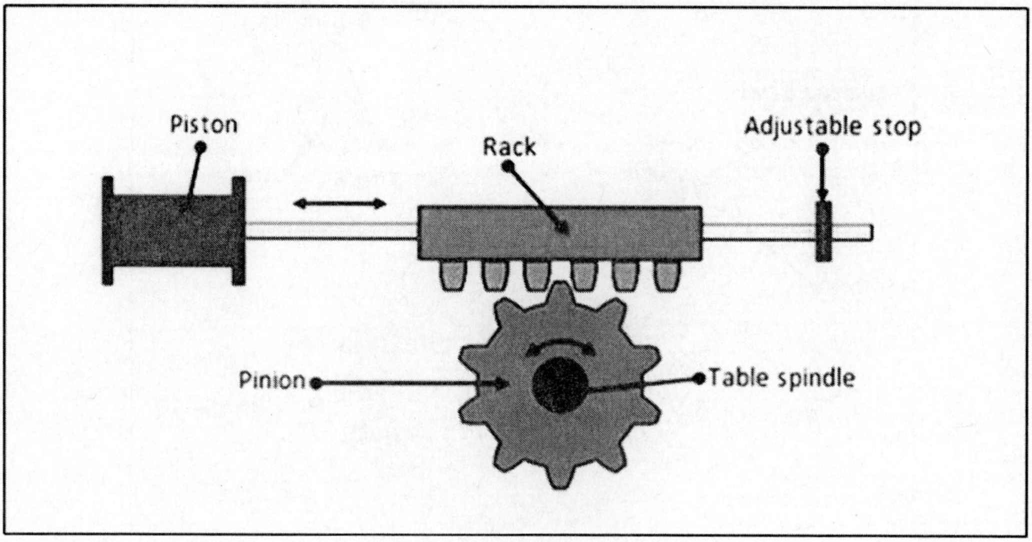

Fig. 2.12. Rack and Pinion

2.8.2.2. Ratchet and Pawl

A ratchet allows movement in one direction of rotation or linear motion but restricts it in the other. The parts of a wrench include a gearwheel and a pawl, which is a spring-loaded finger that revolves to engage the teeth. The spring moves up and over each tooth separately, then, when the teeth move in one direction, it pushes the pawl back into the depression before the subsequent tooth. When the pawl or teeth make an angle, this happens. The pawl strikes a tooth due to its angle, which stops it from moving further in the direction of the moving teeth. The pictorial representation below demonstrates the driving mechanism. Schematic view of ratchet and pawl is shown in Fig. 2.13.

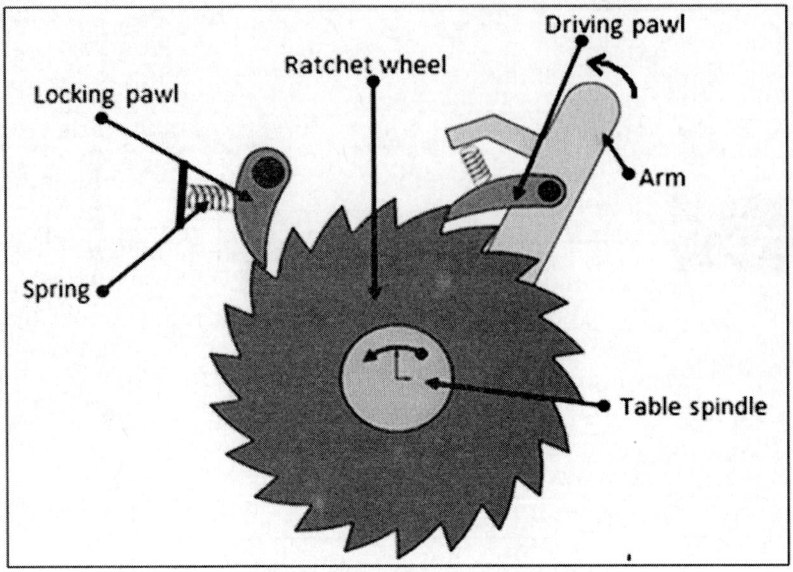

Fig. 2.13. Ratchet and Pawl

2.8.2.3. Geneva Mechanism

Linear motion is converted to rotating motion by the two previous mechanics. The Geneva mechanism uses a continuously rotating motor to index the table. The table moves one-sixth of a turn with each turn of the driver if the driven member has six slots for a six-station dial indexing mechanism. The table moves since the driver only spins it halfway. The table indexes for a six-slotted driven member when the driver rotates 120°. Take up the remaining 240°. For a driven member with four slots, the dwell is 270° and the index ratio is 90°. A basic Geneva mechanism is frequently affordable and simple to design and build because all of the pieces are made up of circular arcs and straight lines rather than curved shapes. The disadvantage of using the standard Geneva mechanism is the noticeable effect caused by the acceleration discontinuity at the beginning and end positions when the driving crank links and separates from the wheel slot. Geneva mechanism is shown in Fig. 2.14.

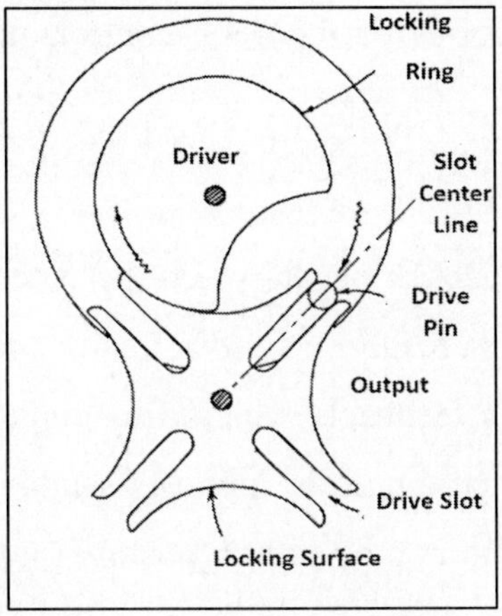

Fig. 2.14. Geneva Mechanism

2.9. Feedback Systems and Control

Feedback measures and compares the control system's output to the input reference signal. To ensure that the system is error-free, the controller that communicates the result measures the divergence between the two. An error signal generated by a feedback loop drives the system by sampling its output signal and delivering it to the input. These systems are typically used to compare the applied input to the obtained result in order offer more accurate feedback. A control system that uses feedback becomes less sensitive to undesired both internal and external disturbances. The schematic view of feedback systems and control is illustrated in Fig. 2.15.

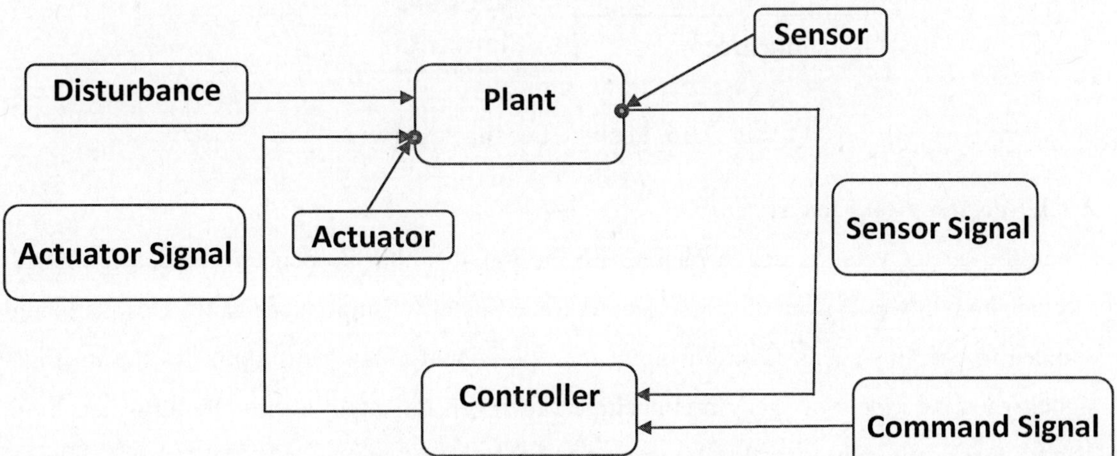

Fig. 2.15. Feedback Control System

There are only two basic categories of feedback control: negative feedback and positive feedback.

2.9.1. Positive Feedback System

A process known as positive feedback occurs when the outcomes of one activity prompt a subsequent action to take place in a feedback system. Positive feedback encourages an activity to get started instead of negative feedback, which discourages it from doing such. Positive feedback control of an operational amplifier involves sending just a fraction of the output voltage signals at V_{out} back to the non-inverting (positive) input terminals via the feedback resistor. If the input voltage V_{in} is positive, an operational amplifier boosts the positive signal to make the output more positive. The feedback network converts a portion of this output voltage back into input voltage. As a result, the input voltage becomes positive in magnitude, causing an even greater output voltage, and so on. Finally, the output reaches saturation in the positive supply channel. Positive feedback system is shown in Fig. 2.16.

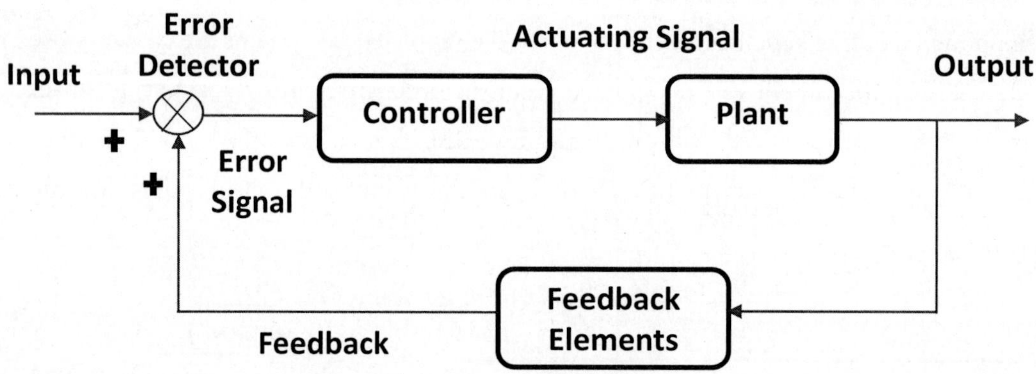

Fig. 2.16. Positive Feedback System

2.9.2. Negative Feedback System

When the output value is not in phase with the initial input, the negative feedback control mechanism removes it from the preset value. Rejecting criticism reduces gains. Despite being coupled to the amplifier's inverted input, the operational component amplifies the positive signal when the input voltage Vin is positive. However, its output eventually turns negative. The feedback system uses feedback resistors to return preset percentages of the output voltage to the input. When the negative feedback signal reduces the input voltage, the output voltage also decreases. The schematic view of negative feedback system is shown in Fig. 2.17.

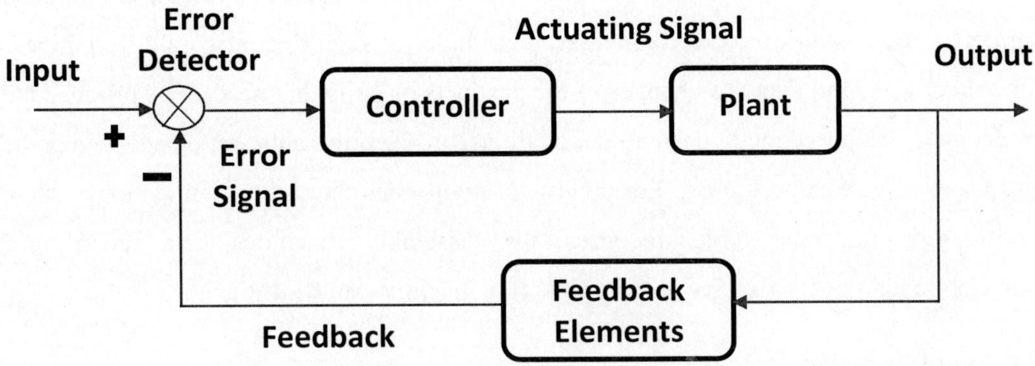

Fig. 2.17. Negative Feedback System

Advantage of Feedback Control System

- It's a pretty basic strategy that adjusts for any disruption.
- Using the set point, the controller modifies the controlled variable.
- The disturbance that enters the process doesn't concern the feedback control circuit.

Disadvantage of Feedback Control System

- Corrective action is not initiated until the disruption changes the process and generates an error signal.
- The feedback controllers modify their output whenever the specified level and measurement coincide.

2.10. Modular and reconfigurable machines

The basic idea underlying flexibility in the field of mechanical engineering is to divide large machines into modules that can be independently built with increasing numbers of identical elements. The combination of these components provides coverage for a wide range of machines. Due to the resulting economies of scale, modular machines may be made more quickly and economically. They can also be adjusted more easily and put to use faster. To ensure that the units may be linked quickly and simply, standardised interfaces are required.

These include mechanical connections, as well as those needed for pressurised air transmission and power distribution connection.

When demand shifts, a reconfigurable machine's structure can be modified to provide alternative functionalities or a little increase in production rate. Reconfigurable machines are primarily designed to adapt to changes in the products or parts that need to be produced. The part geometry, required methods, material qualities, production volume and pace, and possible adjustments are all considered. For many different manufacturing applications, such as reconfigurable machine tools, reconfigurable assembly machines, and reconfigurable inspection machines for fixtures, a reconfigurable machine can be designed.

2.11. Adaptive machine controls

When a controller needs to adjust to a controlled system with varying or unknown parameters, they employ adaptive control, which is related to a control technique. The term "adaptive control" refers to a group of methods that enable the real-time adjustment of control parameter values. This ensures precise tracking of the variables that are under control even in situations when the plant variables are uncertain or fluctuate over time. This control method has two-time scales: the fast time, which is the feedback loop, and the slow time, which is the control variable change that influences the automated actions. This type of control is distinct from other non-linear controls.

Adaptive control is the ability of a controller to modify its control approach in response to a controlled environment whose initial characteristics are unknown or change over time. Adaptive control might not require prior knowledge of limitations associated with these inconsistent or time-varying variables, as compared to robust control. Robust control ensures that, provided changes fall within predefined bounds, the control theory need not be modified, whereas adaptive control concerns about the control theory improving on its own. For example, the usage of fuel causes an aircraft's mass to gradually decrease while it is in flight; hence, a control law that can adapt to these changing conditions is required.

2.11.1. Classification of Adaptive Control Systems

There are two kinds of adaptive control systems:

Indirect Adaptive Control

Direct Adaptive Control

2.11.1.1 Indirect Adaptive Control

A system model's parameters are estimated using the parameter modification technique. The controller parameters are computed as a solution to a design problem using the estimated parameters, presuming that the process parameters are satisfactory. In this instance, a plant parameter estimation method can be identified. The parameter establishing technique specifies exactly how the controller's parameters needed to be set. This implies that the controller's parameters have to be defined in terms of the parameters of the system model. It should be noted that while indirect schemes are more adaptable and provide the use of different

identification techniques and the building of a specific controller depending on the data gathered, direct adaptive schemes necessitate the application of specific plant features. Indirect adaptive control system is depicted in Fig. 2.18.

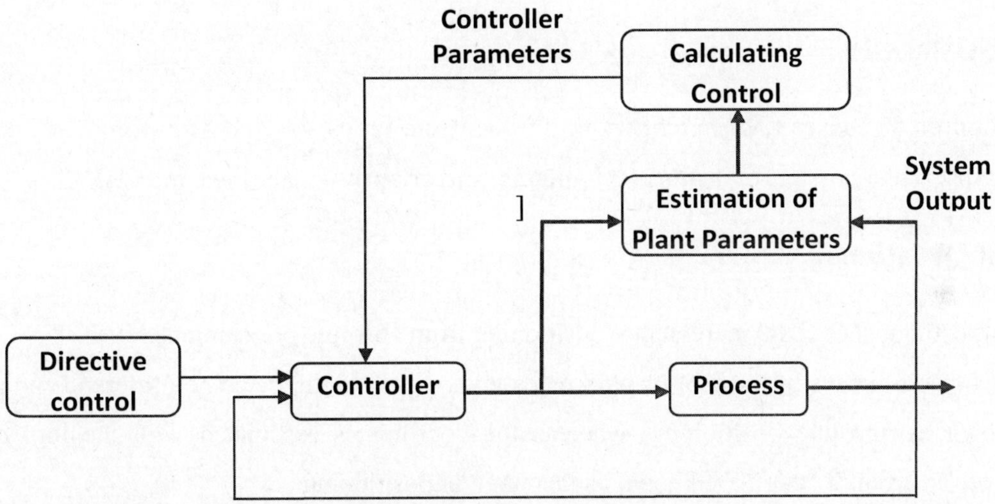

Fig. 2.18. Indirect Adaptive Control

2.11.1.2. Direct Adaptive Control

The parameter establishing technique specifies exactly how the controller's parameters needed to be set. This implies that the controller's parameters have to be defined in terms of the parameters of the system model. It should be noted that while indirect schemes are more adaptable and provide the use of different identification techniques and the building of a specific controller depending on the data gathered, direct adaptive schemes necessitate the application of specific plant features. Direct adaptive control is represented in Fig. 2.19.

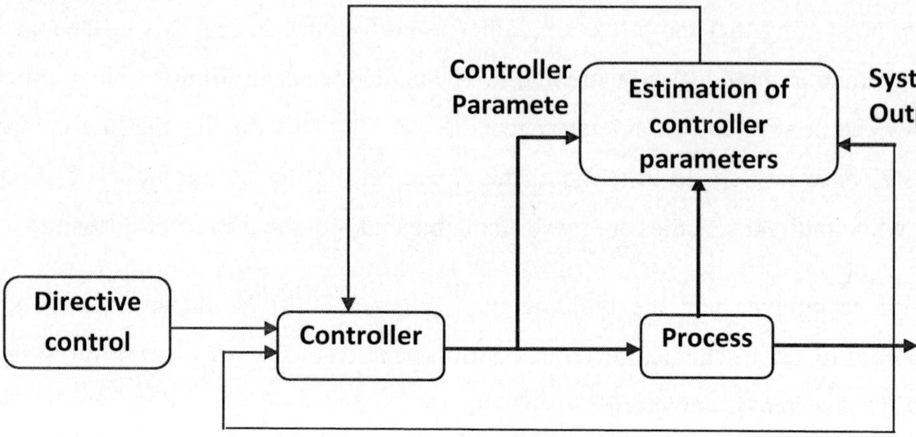

Fig. 2.19. Direct Adaptive Control

UNIT SUMMARY

This chapter discusses CNC machines and its various types, as well as automated flow lines, work part transfer, transfer mechanisms, and adaptive machine controls.

Solved Questions

1. What distinguishes CNC incremental positioning from absolute positioning?

Ans1. The coordinates of the tool or workpiece with regard to the machine's reference point are known as absolute positioning, whereas the coordinates associated with the tool or workpiece's current location are known as incremental positioning.

2. How does backlash in CNC machining get defined?

Ans2. If a CNC machine's mechanical components' little play or clearance is not sufficiently compensated for, it can lead to errors. This phenomenon is known as backlash.

3. In CNC machining, how may tool life be maximised?

Ans3. Tool life can be extended in CNC machining by employing coolants, choosing the right cutting tools, fine-tuning cutting parameters, and adhering to recommended tool maintenance procedures.

4. What is the precise purpose of a CNC cylindrical grinding machine?

Ans4. A computer-controlled device that precisely grinds workpieces' cylindrical surfaces or diameters is called a CNC cylindrical grinding machine.

5. What precisely does a designer of CNC machines do?

Ans5. It is the responsibility of a CNC machine designer to design and develop CNC machines while keeping performance, efficiency, ergonomics, and safety in mind.

6. What specific uses are there for a CNC laser cutting machine?

Ans6. A laser cutting CNC machine efficiently cuts a variety of materials, including acrylic, metallic material, and wood, using a powerful laser beam that is controlled by a computer.

7. What does an inspector for CNC machines do?

Ans7. A CNC machine inspector is in charge of checking completed workpieces to make sure they meet all standards and to confirm their dimensions and quality.

Exercises

1. Explain three types of automated flow line. Write down its selection criteria.
2. What do you mean by positive and negative feedback system? Explain briefly.
3. Classify adaptive control systems.
4. Explain briefly linear and rotary transfer mechanism.
5. Explain Geneva mechanism with the help of neat sketch.
6. Explain briefly different methods of work-part transport.
7. Explain rotary configuration with the help of neat sketch. Why rotary configuration work-part transfer rate is higher as compared to other configurations?
8. Write down advantages and disadvantages of feedback control system.

Multiple Choice Questions

1. What is a control system?

   a. A control system is one in which the output is determined by modifying the input.

   b. A control system is a device that does not manage or regulate the behaviour of other devices via control loops.

   c. The control system functions as a feedback mechanism, which can be positive or negative.

   d. A control system regulates input by adjusting output.

2. A control system operating with random, unidentified activities is known as:

   a. Adaptive control system

   b. Stochastic control system

   c. Computer control system

   d. Digital data system

3. Which of the following describes a modern control system's feature?

   a. Correct power level

   b. No oscillation

   c. Quick response

   d. Accuracy

4. Which of the following elements is not employed in an automated control system?

   a. Final control element

   b. Sensor

   c. Oscillator

   d. Error detector

5. Which of the following statements about any closed loop system is true?

   a. Only one of the static error co-efficient has a finite non-zero value

   b. All the co-efficient can have zero value

   c. All the co-efficient are always non-zero

   d. All of the mentioned

6. The feedback control system's output has to be a function of

   a. Output and feedback signal

   b. Input and feedback signal

   c. Reference input

   d. Reference output

7. Which of the following is not a CNC machine component?

   a. Milling

   b. Computer

   c. Control box

   d. NC program

8. Which of the following does not constitute CNC software?

   a. Machine sequencing software

   b. Operating system

   c. Machine interface software

   d. Application software

9. What mode switch position allows for the execution of a single CNC command?

   a. Jog

   b. Auto

   c. MDI (manual data Input)

   d. Edit

10. The button that activates the CNC program after a temporary standstill is:

    a. Reset

    b. Emergency Stop

    c. Coolant On

    d. Cycle Start

11. Which of the following modern CNC characteristics gives it an advantage over earlier numerical control machines?

    a. Reprogramming ability

    b. Capability to deal with product variety

    c. Adaptive control

    d Need of lesser human assistance

12. Which of these parts makes up the machine control unit in CNC machines?
    a. I/O Interface
    b. Scanners
    c. Plotters
    d. Processing equipment

13. Which of the following parts makes up a CNC's central processing unit?
    a. Read Only Memory
    b. Arithmetic Logic Unit
    c. Secondary memory
    d. Operating System Unit

14. In a control system the controller's output is supplied to:
    a. Amplifier
    b. Sensor
    c. Final control element
    d. Comparator

15. Which of the following is likely to be a problem with an excessively noisy control system?
    a. Oscillations
    b. Saturation in amplifying stages
    c. Loss of gain
    d. Vibrations

16. ______ allows the user to create and modify part programmes.
    a. Control program
    b. Executive program
    c. Machine interface program
    d. Editor

17. Consider the following statements with respect to the feedback of the control systems.
    a. Feedback can improve stability or be harmful to stability if it is not properly applied.
    b. Feedback can always improve stability
    c. In many situations the feedback can reduce the effect of noise and disturbance on system performance.

d. In general the sensitivity of the system gain of a feedback system of a parameter variation depends on where the parameter is located.

Choose the appropriate answer

a, b, c and d only

a, b and c only

a, c and d only

a, b and d only

18. A CNC part programme can be changed while it's still stored in the memory of the machine control unit.

a. True

b. False

Answers for multiple choice questions:

Keys for multiple choice questions: 1(a), 2(b), 3(b), 4(c), 5(a), 6(b), 7(d), 8(a), 9(c), 10(d), 11(c), 12(a), 13(b), 14(c), 15(b), 16(d), 17 (a, c, d only), 18 (a)

KNOW MORE

For more information related to this topic scan the QR code,

OR

Type this link in your browser

https://ufile.io/y8gp0xbo

References

1. https://archive.nptel.ac.in/courses/112/105/112105211/

2. https://www.cncsourced.com/guides/what-is-cnc-complete-cnc-guide/

3. https://cncmachines.com/what-is-a-cnc-machine

4. Mikell P. Groover, Automation, Production Systems and Computer Integrated Manufacturing, Fourth Edition, Pearson. USA (2015).

3 Automated Assembly Systems

UNIT SPECIFICS

This chapter presents a brief description of automated assembly and transfer systems, which are frequently used in industries.

RATIONALE

Automated assembly systems are an integral part of automation industries. Its knowledge is very much essential for professional, working in automation industries.

PRE-REQUISITE

Knowledge of automated assembly systems.

UNIT OUTCOMES

List of outcomes of this unit is as follows:

U3-O1: Students should be able to understand the developments of automated systems

U3-O2: Students should be able to understand transfer systems; vibratory and non-vibratory feeders

U3-O3: Students should be able to know about feed tracks, part orienting and placing mechanisms

Unit Outcomes	Expected Mapping with Programme Outcomes (1- Weak Correlation; 2- Medium correlation; 3- Strong Correlation)					
	PO-1	PO-2	PO-3	PO-4	PO-5	PO-6
U3-01	3	1	3	1	1	2
U3-02	3	3	2	2	2	3
U3-03	3	3	1	2	1	3

An overview of historical advancements and the selection of assembly methods are given in this chapter. This chapter covers the design for automated assembly's evolution and advances.

Readers are given further information regarding vibratory and non-vibratory feeders and transfer systems. This chapter provides an overview of automated assembly, automated flow lines, automated transfer systems, and vibratory and non-vibratory feeders. Machinery that is modular and adaptable makes up its core component. A review of feed tracks and part orienting and placement mechanisms brings the unit to a close.

3.1. Historical developments

Modern manufacturing systems will demand greater flexibility in terms of planning, process management, product design, and process scheduling. This could be accomplished by combining hardware and software frameworks that translate assembly system decisions into indications that are sent through networks of connections for implementation. Automation industries have yet to reach this degree of production technology. However, the desire to achieve this goal is reflected in the term "intelligent systems," which obtained importance in the late 1980s. The intelligence required to automate assembly methods was not established during our early attempts to build such sophisticated systems, known as knowledge-driven systems.

The limits of these systems compel researchers to investigate new technologies. Artificial neural networks, which transformed the design of intelligent systems, arose in the mid-1980s as a novel approach to addressing scientific and engineering challenges. They introduced the concept of learning and adaptability, which evolved as a solution to a number of engineering issues in manufacturing, including automated assembly. Development of automated assembly systems can be classified into following: fixed, high-volume design, flexible, general-purpose system and single, flexible, programmable robot.

A machine with a fixed, high-volume design is one that is specifically made for producing a single product. Although all of the fixtures and work heads are dedicated to this function, only minor modifications to the product can be accepted or adapted. Strict tolerances are set up, and the feeding devices and their holding fixtures are designed to ensure that the parts that need to be assembled have a low defect rate.

The fixed, high-volume machines are intended to operate quickly, therefore the cycle time for each machine operation, as well as the rate of production, are preset.

The system can adapt to minor modifications in the appearance and design of products because it is made for medium-volume activities. Adjustable parts publications containers, cartridges for printing, or rolls that are readily available to the work head and packed are examples of

such adaptable, medium-volume activities; these instruments are set up and configured to be taken and utilised on an intermittent basis. Other prominent characteristics of the adaptable system include robotic arms, end effectors, that programmed indexed rotary table feeders, and automatic tool changers. Due to this versatility, only one workstation can do numerous assembly tasks, enabling the system output to meet a lower demand pace. Higher spans along with more activities needed also extend assembly times, which lowers rates of production.
The single, flexible, programmable robot is a notable exception to this ruling, as it is employed for low-volume, repetitive assembly and requires accurate, error-free functioning. It varies from the flexibility variant stated above solely in that an automated arm integrated into a medium-volume operation isn't the same as a single machine performing a series of assembling steps in a somewhat distinct or semi-isolated setting. The single robot can also be mounted on rails to expand its area of motion or reach; however, this increases cycle time.

3.2. Automated Assembly Systems

The process of using robotic and automated machines to complete multiple tasks in a production line or unit is known as automated assembly. An automated assembly system combines several pieces into a single unit, that can be a final object or a subassembly, using a series of automated operations. To create a new entity that can be assembled or disassembled, two or more separate components are joined together in an assembly. Due to the economic significance of assembly, robotic technologies are frequently used. Fixed automation is suitable for large manufacturing of relatively basic products. Robots are typically at an advantage in rapid-production events since they can't operate at the same rapid pace as fixed-automated systems. The most appealing utilization of robotic machines for assembly is to create a variety of comparable designs within the identical job unit or production line.

Examples of these items comprise motors for electricity, fragile equipment, along with other mechanical and electrical devices.

Reason for automated assembly

- Increased consumer demand for products.
- Robust design for the product.
- The assembly consists of only a few components.

- The item is intended for automated assembly.
- When performing repetitive operations, automated assembly systems greatly minimise the requirement for human interaction.
- They improve the quality of the product by reducing fatigue-related errors that arise during repetitive tasks.
- Stable task completion guarantees steady production.
- Automation boosts competitiveness and lowers labour expenses.
- Consider in terms of kinematics, accessibility, and cargo systems.

3.3. Design for automated assembly

Principles and guidelines for incorporating automated assembly into product design.

Minimize the amount of assembly needed: This idea can be implemented in design by consolidating tasks that have previously been finished by various product parts into a single part. This idea is demonstrated by the usage of polymer parts in place of sheet metal. A polymer component with a more complex geometry could take the place of several metal components. In many cases, the obvious increased cost of the polymer component is probably balanced by any assembly time decrease.

Make use of modular design: In automated assembly, the number of distinctive assembly steps that a single automated system can finish will grow, resulting in an increase in the system's downtime. To mitigate this downside, the product's design must be modular; every section might require a maximum of 12 to 13 components assembled on a single assembly system. Moreover, the subassembly should be built using a foundation element that other parts are built around.

Minimise the quantity of fasteners utilised in components: Using snap fits and associated features to include the fastening mechanism into the component design rather than utilizing individual screws, nuts, and other fasteners. Furthermore, when designing product components, make sure that multiple components are fastened simultaneously instead of one at a time.

Minimise the required direction of access: This principle argues that new components should be added to an existing subassembly with as few orientations as possible. In a perfect environment, every component would be mounted vertically from above. The design of the subassembly part simply implies conformity.

Demand premium-grade components: For the automated assembly system to function optimally, the components inserted at each workstation must be of a consistent high standard. The automated system experiences delay due to blockages in the feeding and assembly processes caused by deficient components.

Minimizes the requirement for numerous components to be handled simultaneously:

The preferred approach in automated assembly equipment design is to segregate tasks at several stations rather than handling and fastening numerous parts at a single workstation.

3.4. Parts Transfer System

It is necessary to devise a way to send the components to the assembly workhead in each of the combinations mentioned above. It will also be covered in more detail below.

3.4.1. Components of the system for delivering parts

The base element is sometimes placed into a work carrier or pallet fixture at the system's starting station, whereas a workstation performs one or both of the following tasks in each of the aforementioned configurations: A fastening or joining operation carried out at the station and a component delivered to the assembly work head that is fastened to the existing base part in front of the work head are the two permanent methods of attaching components to the existing base part. When using a one-station assembly system, the single station performs these

The hardware components of the parts transfer system typically include the following examples as shown in Fig. 3.1.

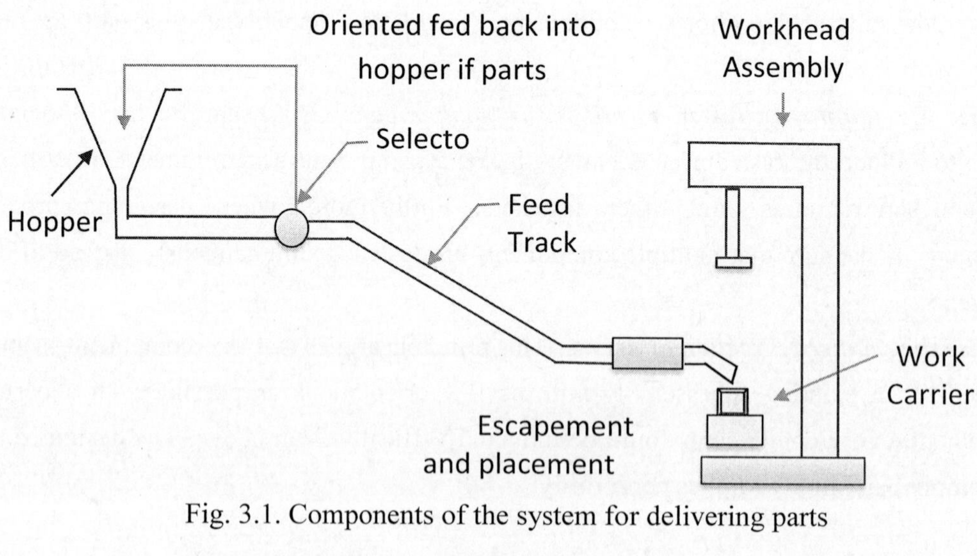

Fig. 3.1. Components of the system for delivering parts

3.4.1.1. Hopper: At the workstation, parts are inserted into this container. Every type of part has its own hopper. Usually, the parts are added to the hopper in large quantities. This indicates that the components' orientation within the hopper is randomized.

3.4.1.2. Parts feeder: This is a device that takes parts out of the hopper one by one so they can be sent to the assembly work head. A single operational mechanism frequently serves as both the hopper and the components feeder. One of the most prevalent types of hopper-feeder combinations is the vibratory bowl feeder shown in Fig. 3.2.

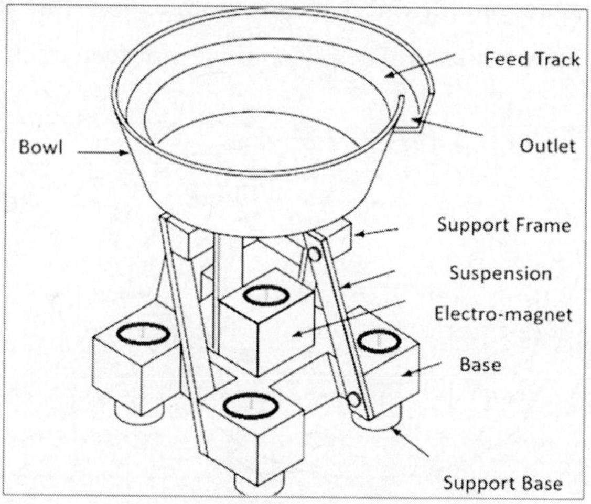

Fig 3.2. vibratory bowl feeder

3.4.1.3. Selector or Orientor: The proper alignment of the parts for the assembly workhead is determined by these delivery system components. A selector functions as a filter, permitting those components that are oriented correctly to pass through. Incorrectly aligned components are rejected and sent back to the hopper. An orientor is a tool that reorients components that were initially improperly oriented while permitting pans that are correctly aligned to pass through. Multiple selection and orientor schemes are depicted in the Fig. 3.3. Devices for orienting and selecting are frequently integrated into hopper-feeder systems.

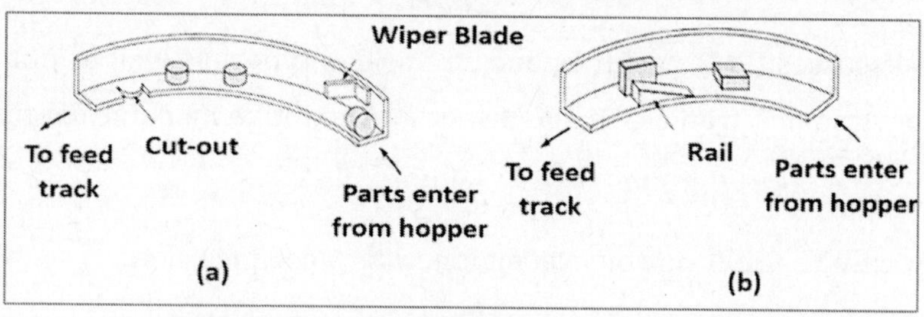

Fig. 3.3. Selector (a) and Orientor (b)

3.4.1.4. Feed tracks, part orienting and placing mechanisms track: The prior parts of the supply system and the assembly work head are frequently set at a certain separation from one another. A feed track is used to move the parts from the hopper and parts feeder to the assembly work head location, ensuring that the components are orientated correctly the entire time. Powered and gravity are the two main categories into which feed tracks fall. Gravity feed tracks are the most common. On this type, the parts feeder and hopper are positioned above the work head. Gravity transports the components to the work head. The powered feed track uses vibratory action, air pressure, or other mechanisms to urge the pieces to travel down the feed track towards the assembly work head. The pictorial view of feed track is shown in Fig. 3.4.

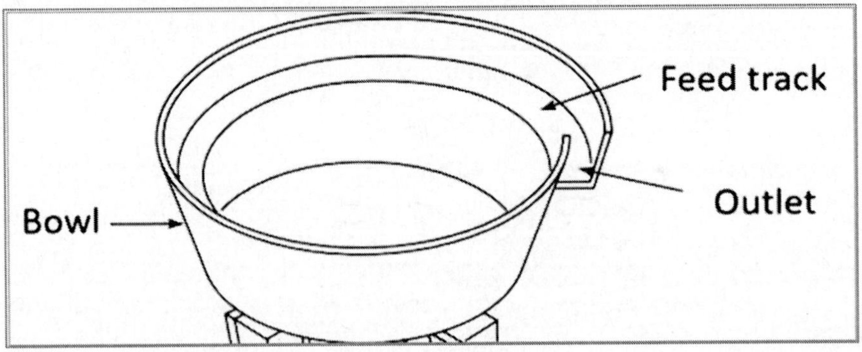

Fig. 3.4. Feed Track

3.4.1.5. Escapement and placement device:

Components are removed from the feed track by the escapement at intervals that match the assembly work head's cycle time. During assembly procedures, the placement device precisely aligns the component at the workstation. Occasionally, these parts are integrated into a single functional mechanism. There are situations in which they can operate on their own.

UNIT SUMMARY

This chapter discusses CNC machines and its various types, as well as automated flow lines, work part transfer, transfer mechanisms, and adaptive machine controls.

Solved Examples

1. In assembly activities, how do you guarantee accuracy and precision?

Ans1. Precision and accuracy are required throughout assembly activities, necessitating careful planning, rigorous adherence to procedures, and regular quality checks. In the beginning, I would ensure that I understood the component's descriptions and assembly instructions. This eliminates the potential of errors and ensures that I fully understand what needs to be done. I would use the appropriate tools and methods throughout assembly to ensure that each part was properly assembled. Torque wrenches, for example, are useful for precisely adjusting screws and nuts. Throughout the process, periodical checks are necessary. Verification of efforts allows me to catch faults prior they become significant. Finally, keep a nice and clean environment. It reduces the potential of errors and distractions, allowing you to maintain your focus on attaining correct outcomes.

2. What plan do you have in place to make sure the workplace is organized and safe?
Ans2. The strategy includes proactive actions to ensure a safe and clean work environment. I believe it is critical to maintain regular cleaning schedules, keep all equipment in good functioning order, and address any possible dangers promptly. I also appreciate personal protective equipment and ensure that it is used properly at all times. Furthermore, I would foster a culture of safety among my coworkers by being open about safety protocols. This includes reporting any flaws as soon as possible so they can be corrected before they cause harm. Essentially, it boils down to practicing caution, accepting responsibility, and cultivating a feeling of community in terms of workplace hygiene and safety.

3. How do you ensure that the constructed product satisfies all specifications and quality standards?
Ans3. To ensure that the finished product meets all specifications and quality standards, I start by carefully studying the assembly instructions and blueprints. This helps me understand exactly what to expect in terms of the ultimate output. Throughout the assembly process, I use precision equipment to assure accurate measurements and fit. Regular inspections at various stages of assembly are also required to identify potential issues early on.

Exercises

1. Explain the working of feed track with neat sketch.
2. What do you mean by design for automated assembly?

3. Write down the components of the system for delivering parts and explain any three of them.
4. Differentiate between vibratory and non-vibratory feeders.
5. Explain different types of assembly methods.
6. Define briefly part orienting and placing mechanisms.
7. Write down the historical development of automated assembly system.
8. Write down the significance of escapement and placement device.

Multiple Choice Questions

1. What is the automated assembly system's primary use for a vibratory bowl feeder?

   a. Transport workpieces between machines

   b. Orient and feed component parts c. Store components for future use

   d. Inspect finished items

2. Which type of feeder is typically used when an arbitrarily categorized bulk pack of small components needs to be fed into a different device one at a time, orientated in a specific direction?

   a. Feeder options include vibratory bowls

   b. Reciprocating tube hoppers

   c. Rotary discs

   d. Electromagnetic feeders

3. What kind of material is commonly utilized for the bowl in a vibratory bowl feeder?

   a. Aluminium

   b. Stainless Steel

   c. Polyamide

   d. All of the aforementioned

4. Which kind of non-vibratory feeder is frequently utilized with rotary transfer mechanisms and linear travel?

   a. Reciprocating fork hopper feeder

   b. External gate hopper feeder

   c. Centerboard hopper feeder

   d. Reciprocating tube hopper feeder

5. A pair is considered a kinematic pair if the relative motion between its connections is:
   a. Completely or successfully constrained
   b. Not constrained
   c. Unrelated
   d. None of the aforementioned

6. What kind of feeding may a feed mechanism facilitate?
   a. Automatic
   b. Manual
   c. Automatic and manual
   d. None of the above

7. A kinematic pair is one in which the relative motion between its links is:
   a. Completely or successfully constrained
   b. Not constrained
   c. Unrelated
   d. None of the above

8. Which of the following is not a common input device in a control system?
   a. Sensors
   b. Actuators
   c. Timers
   d. Speakers

9. In automated assembly, which of the following claims regarding part orientation is true?
   a. Good assembly processes do not require part orientation
   b. Part orientation can be easily changed by hand by human personnel
   c. It is easy to teach robots to replicate human-level dexterity for part orientation
   d. Expensive customization is not necessary for assembly robots to ensure consistent part alignment

10. What is the main benefit of automated assembly in the manufacturing industry?
   a. Lower labour expenses
   b. Higher human mistake rates
   c. Slower production speed
   d. More adaptability

11. What type of control system uses a set of pre-programmed instructions to control a process?
    a. Sequential control
    b. Programmable Logic Control
    c. Proportional control
    d. Integral control

12. What does the word "pick-and-place" mean in automated assembly?
    a. Picking a random item from a bin
    b. Moving a part to a certain location
    c. Choosing the most expensive component
    d. Ignoring the damaged parts

13. What kind of sensor is often used in automated assembly systems to detect the presence of components?
    a. Temperature
    b. Proximity
    c. Sound
    d. Taste

14. Which software programme manages drafting, production, design, analysis, and data entry?
    a. Graphics software
    b. Programming software
    c. Operating software
    d. Application software

15. Which of the following describes the chemical qualities of good product material?
    a. Corrosion
    b. Surface treatment
    c. Oxidation
    d. A combination of the three

16. What is the primary purpose of automated manufacturing?
    a. Increase manual labour requirements
    b. Improve product quality and efficiency
    c. Reduce product diversity
    d. Increase energy usage

17. What exactly does 'PLC' stand for in automation?
    a. Programmable logic controller
    b. Personal computer
    c. Portable logic circuit
    d. Programmable linear conveyor

18. Which device is most commonly linked with automation.
    a. CNC machines
    b. Flexible manufacturing
    c. Graphics workstations
    d. Robots

Answers for multiple choice questions:

Keys for multiple choice questions: 1(b), 2(a), 3(b), 4(d), 5(a), 6(c), 7(a), 8(d), 9(d), 10(a), 11(b), 12(b), 13(b), 14(d), 15(d), 16(b), 17(a), 18(d)

KNOW MORE

For more information related to this topic scan the QR code,

OR

Type this link in your browser

https://ufile.io/wz29agxc

References

1. https://onlinecourses.nptel.ac.in/noc22_me50/preview
2. https://onlinecourses.nptel.ac.in/noc21_me120/preview
3. Mikell P. Groover, Automation, Production Systems and Computer Integrated Manufacturing, Fourth Edition, Pearson. USA (2015).
4. https://onlinecourses.nptel.ac.in/noc22_me50/preview
5. https://www.feederuniversity.com/modules/vibratory-feeder-basics

4 Factory Automation

UNIT SPECIFICS

A basic overview of factory automation, which is in great demand across industries, is discussed in this chapter.

RATIONALE

In the manufacturing industry, factory automation is akin to a revolution and its knowledge is always beneficial, if one must know how to implement these.

PRE-REQUISITE

Knowledge of automation.

UNIT OUTCOMES

List of outcomes of this unit is as follows:

U4-O1: Students should be able to understand the lean manufacturing

U4-O2: Students should be able to know about analysis of transfer lines and automated flow lines

U4-O3: Students should be able to brief about partial and full automation

Unit Outcomes	Expected Mapping with Programme Outcomes *(1- Weak Correlation; 2- Medium correlation; 3- Strong Correlation)*					
	PO-1	PO-2	PO-3	PO-4	PO-5	PO-6
U4-O1	3	1	3	1	1	2
U4-O2	3	3	2	2	2	3
U4-O3	3	3	1	2	1	3

An overview of automation scalability, lean manufacturing, and analysis of transfer lines without storage. This chapter defines average production time, production rate, and line efficiency. The examination of transfer lines with and without storage is covered in this chapter. Additional details regarding partial and full automation are provided to the readers. An overview of the common automation types utilized in industries is given in this chapter.

4.1. Factory Automation: Lean manufacturing, Automation scalability (fixed, programmable, flexible and reconfigurable); Design and analysis of automated flow lines; Average production time, production rate, line efficiency; Analysis of transfer lines without storage; Partial and full automation.

4.1.1. Lean Manufacturing

A production strategy known as "lean manufacturing" is based on the concept of optimizing outputs while minimizing waste in the manufacturing process. According to the lean methodology, anything which fails to provide worth that customers are ready to pay for as waste. This is performed by eliminating waste from the production cycle using lean principles, techniques, and technologies. The Toyota Production System was the first to use the lean manufacturing technique, which transformed the company's manufacturing processes before spreading across various countries.

The primary goal of lean manufacturing is to remove waste caused by various supply chain activities; however, it is crucial to realise that waste can take several forms. In a larger sense, industrial waste might refer to the use of materials, power utilisation, but the term lean manufacturing specifically relates to the effective circulation of goods from the manufacturing process to delivery to their intended customers.

Objectives of Lean Manufacturing

Following are the objectives of Lean Manufacturing:

4.1.1.1. Improving Utilisation of Resources

In order to attain maximum efficiency, lean manufacturing aims to eradicate wasteful use of resources, minimize goods stocks, and enhance production procedures. In addition to helping companies increase revenue, this helps them reduce waste and cut costs so they can price their products properly for the customer. Within this methodology, waste encompasses both the physical wastage of raw materials and the unseen waste of resources, such as staff time and effort.

It might also be the result of poor production quality, excessive raw material processing, or ineffective transportation.

4.1.1.2. Enhancing the Level of Performance

Lean management aims for continuous development, which aids in providing customers with the greatest quality goods. Furthermore, this can improve the process of goods development and innovation. Organizations can re-evaluate their procedures after adopting changes to find methods that will enhance operations even more and deliver a superior experience to their customers.

4.1.1.3. Improving Production Efficiency and Capability

Increased production flexibility helps an organization to reach more customers without expanding its production facilities or spending significant expenses. An organization's capacity for production increases with its adaptability. Lean manufacturing is an approach which promotes collaboration at all stages of the manufacturing process in order to maximize production.

4.1.1.4. Minimizing expenditures

Reduction of waste, more efficient use of time, and optimum production capacity all contribute to lower manufacturing costs. This helps businesses to maintain their competitiveness in the market by providing higher-quality items at more affordable pricing. Also, it enables companies to boost revenue, improve customer support, and allocate additional resources for product development.

4.1.1.5. Strengthening the work environment

Productivity is increased and the work environment is improved through lean manufacturing. It creates a working environment where people are happy and at ease in their work. Additionally, lean manufacturing promotes increased safety and regulatory compliance in manufacturing facilities, creating safer working conditions for staff members.

4.2. The five pillars of lean manufacturing

These are the five pillars of lean manufacturing:

4.2.1. Identify Value

Value identification is the first step towards understanding the core idea of customer value evaluation. Value may be discovered by looking at the customer's willingness to spend. Determining if the customer is really in need of something or whether their wants have been disguised is crucial. Often, customers struggle to articulate their demands or wants in a clear and concise manner. This is particularly valid when novel goods or procedures are employed.

4.2.2. Design a Value Flow Chart

It is simple to determine the benefits that individuals value utilising a range of methods, such as web data analysis, questionnaires, interviews, and demographic information. should employ both qualitative and quantitative methods to determine precisely what clients want, what they expect from the items provided, and how much they are ready to spend.

4.2.3. Establish Flow

Following the elimination of waste products from the value flow, the next stage is to ensure that the remaining operations work smoothly and without interruption or delay. Breaking down processes, reorganizing manufacturing processes, spreading responsibilities, forming cross-functional groups, and educating staff members to be highly competent and adaptable are all strategies to ensure that value-added tasks are carried out effectively.

4.2.4. Develop a pull system

Inventory is regarded as one of the biggest wastes in any industrial system. The goal of a pull-based system is to reduce inventory and work-in-process items while preserving the accessibility of information and resources required to support effective work flow. In other words, just-in-time manufacturing and delivery - where items are created in precisely the right quantities and at precisely the right times is made possible by a pull-based system. The needs of end users are always taken into consideration while developing pull-based solutions. Working backwards through the manufacturing chain and sticking to the value stream, you can ensure that the commodities produced can match consumer needs.

4.2.5. Strive for Excellence

Waste is prevented by completing the first four steps: identifying value, designing a value flow chart, establishing flow, and developing a pull mechanism. However, the fifth stage in attaining perfection is the most crucial of all. It integrates Lean ideas and continuous process improvement into the organization's culture. Every employee should aim for perfection while delivering items based on consumer needs. The corporation should be a learning organisation that strives to improve itself every day.

4.3. Automation Scalability

Automation Scalability refers to an organization's ability to go from experimenting with automation to adopting it for end-to-end procedures across the business. It involves Robotic and Intelligent Process Automation. Robotic Process Automation is the most fundamental automation level, functioning as the foundation for a variety of activities and frequently originating scalability. Intelligent process automation, which combines robotic process automation, artificial intelligence, and machine learning, is necessary for elevating processes to the next level.

Intelligent and robotic process automation is the only approach to achieve the digital transformation. The ability to learn and enhance decision-making makes these digital robots incredibly beneficial to organisation executives. However, it is not as simple as installing automation and deploying it throughout the organisation. In a scalable environment, automation is utilised to reduce the amount of labour required for oversight and computed scalability. Information Technology struggles to manage data transfers and cloud deployments as workloads increase.

Advantages of Automated Scalability:

The major Advantages of Automated Scalability are as under:

Enhanced Output

Enhanced Precision and Durability

Increased Productivity and Financial Savings

Enhanced Security

Flexibility and Scalability

Enhanced Output

Processes are sped up and manual labour is eliminated with automation. Compared to people, machines and robots can complete tasks more quickly and effectively. Scalable automation leads to higher output and shorter production cycles.

Enhanced Precision and Durability

Automated systems are designed with consistency and accuracy in mind. Higher-quality goods and services are the result of reduced human imperfections and mistakes. Reduced downtime or errors and increased customer satisfaction are the outcomes.

Increased Productivity and Financial Savings

Automation improves process flow, avoids obstructions, and minimizes trash. Automated procedures save money by increasing efficiency and lowering labour expenses. Reduced operational costs add to overall savings.

Enhanced Security

Especially important in hazardous workplace conditions. Replacing workers with machines reduces injuries, accidents, and risks associated with work. The end result is greater safety at work.

Flexibility and Scalability

Automated operations can easily be scaled upward or downward to meet market shifts. Rapid modifications to the level of production and allocation of resources. Flexibility allows organizations to remain compete and meet customer requirements successfully.

4.4. Types of Automation

- Fixed Automation
- Programmable Automation
- Flexible Automation
- Reconfigurable Automation

4.4.1. Fixed Automation

Fixed automation solutions are often simple and designed for a single purpose, such as building a specific product or handling materials. Fixed automated solutions are extremely effective and perfect for automating fixed, repeated manufacturing procedures in massive production lines. In fixed automation systems, internal programming is used. These machines are controlled by software rather than hardware. This makes it difficult to deploy fixed automation systems for a variety of items and manage product changes. For fixed automation, mass producing a specific kind of product or part assembly makes a greater sense. Fixed automated systems are widely used in industrial manufacturing due to the fact that they can enhance efficiency and productivity while reducing labor expenses.

An example of fixed automation is an automated conveyor belt, which is made to move products down an assembly line while functioning as independently while the product is being made. Notable instances of fixed automation are controlled assembly machines that are programmed to assemble particular components or automated spraying processes that provide a final color or sealer to a specific product.

It's a system where the equipment design dictates the sequence in which processing operations are carried out. Sequence operations are usually straightforward. The system's complexity stems from the way several processes are integrated and coordinated into a single piece of machinery. High production rates, a hefty initial investment for specially designed machinery, and little flexibility to adapt to changing product requirements are typical characteristics of fixed automation. Fixed automation is a cost-effective choice for items with high production and demand. The equipment is more cost-effective than other production methods because its high initial cost may be spread across a large number of units. Machining transfer lines and automated assembly are examples of fixed automation.

The following are some examples of fixed automation:

- Automated equipment used for assembling products
- Automating the operations of spraying and painting
- Automation of the chemical process
- Conveying mechanisms for bulky and other kinds of material transfer using machinery
- Components machining transfer lines
- Systems for handling and processing webs for the coating process, metalizing, printing purposes and sealing

Benefits of Fixed Automation

Following are the benefits of fixed automation:

- High volume of production
- Stable and maintained production quality
- High amounts of output
- Stable production quality
- Low production costs
- Robust and basic design

Limitations of Fixed Automation

The major limitations of fixed automation are listed below:

- Modifications are difficult to implement
- Once programming is done, it cannot be changed
- It can only automate simple procedures

4.4.2. Programmable Automation

Programmable automation is the next category of industrial automation. The automated machines group is differentiated by its ability to accomplish the same task in multiple ways. The most common application for programmable automation equipment is in batch production, where equipment is configured to do a specific function on every batch. It can then be set up to take adjustments for a fresh batch after that. Industrial robots with programmable movements and actions, CNC machines that obey computer programmes, and steel rolling mills capable of producing various metal thicknesses are examples of programmable automation.

The basic idea behind programmable automation is the use of programming languages and software to monitor and control automated systems 'operations. In accordance with the requirements and degree of complexity of the automation process, the software used might be something from simple script to intricate algorithms.

Automation of operations that had previously been carried out either manually or with little control is possible because of programmable automation. It enables users to modify and adapt the automated process in response to shifting requirements, producing processes that are adaptive and effective. Because of its flexibility, programmed automation is an essential tool for companies that need to make frequent modifications to their processes. The operation sequence of the production equipment can be altered to accommodate a variety of product designs. A programming is a collection of instructions that the computer is able to read and understand. The operating sequence is under its control. To generate new objects, the machine can be programmed with new programmes. High general-purpose equipment investment, lower production rates than fixed automation, adaptability to changes in product configuration, and batch production appropriateness are some of the traits of programmable automation.

Programmable automated production systems are used in low- and medium-volume production. The products or parts are typically made in batches. For every new batch of a product that is manufactured, the machine instructions must be reprogrammed into the system. It is also necessary to make changes to the machine's physical configuration, including repairing fixtures, loading tools, and entering machine settings. Making the transition requires time. This indicates that for a specific product, the usual cycle consists of a batch production phase that follows a setup and reprogramming phase. Two instances of programmed automation are numerically controlled machine tools and industrial robots.

The following are some examples of programmable automation:

1. Automated numerical control tools
2. Robots in industry
3. Controllers with programmable logic

Benefits of Programmable Automation

Some of major benefits of programmable automation are as under:

- Significantly improves both output and production
- Reduces associated expenses
- Eliminates the need for people to carry out unsafe or monotonous activities shorter scan duration
- Capable of communicating with computers in a manufacturing facility
- Excellent computing capability
- Less time is needed for training

Limitations of Programmable Automation

Following are the limitations of programmable automation:

- More expensive apparatus
- Less units are produced in each production cycle
- It takes time to switch out items or functions
- A moment during transition that is unproductive

4.4.3. Flexible Automation

Flexible automation is an advanced version of programmable automation. Flexible automation features a limited number of devices that enable for automated and rapid improvements to equipment. Flexible automation is required when programming equipment offline; using a computer interface rather than the actual industrial equipment. This eliminates the need to segregate identical products into batches, allowing for the simultaneous manufacturing of a wide range of products. One drawback of programmable automation is the amount of time spent replacing and reprogramming manufacturing machinery for every fresh batch of merchandise. This is an indication of substantial production time spent. It is a development of automation that is programmable. Many items (or parts) can be produced by a flexible automated system with little loss of time during changeovers. While the physical configuration and programming of the system are being done, there is no interruption to production.

There is no longer a requirement for independent batch production because to the system's flexible scheduling and product combinations. When a new part arrives for processing, the physical setup is changed by moving the changeover into place once it has been completed offline. Using pallet fixtures to hold the items and move them to the right location at the jobsite is one way to implement this strategy. In order for these methods to be effective, a flexible automated production system's capacity to produce a given number of components is usually constrained as compared to a system run by programmable automation.

Flexible automation systems usually have the following components:

Parts processing machinery

These operations are partially completed by CNC machining equipment, which is combined with different automated workstations and inspection.

Systems for managing materials

Robots are typically utilized for product loading and unloading in conveyor systems and other related setups that transfer items from one section of a production line to another.

Centralized computer management system

Communications originating from this centralized controller coordinate the operational procedures of various machines and supply components routing information as well as scheduling adjustments inside the material-handling system.

People

Despite the automation at the core of these systems, managing, maintaining, and adjusting processes as needed continues to involve people.

The following are some characteristics of flexible automation:

- Custom-engineered solutions are costly to invest in.
- Continuous manufacture of a variety of products.
- Moderate rates of output.
- Flexibility in addressing modifications to product designs.

4.4.3.1. Examples of Flexible Automation

The following are some examples of Flexible Automation:

1. Flexible automated machinery can be applied by low-volume and high-mix industries with a low cost due to flexible manufacturing procedures.
2. Packaging organizations are using robots more and more frequently.
3. Robots are now capable of handling a wide range of products, including harder to handle ones, in terms of size and shape.
4. This is especially important for cooperative robots that operate in conjunction with humans. They're adaptable to shifting conditions and circumstances and simple to prepare for new jobs.
5. The packaging business has seen a rise in the use of such production automation, including automated packing, source identification, and automated labelling.

4.4.3.2. Benefits of Flexible Automation

There are following benefits of Flexible Automation:

- Flexibility in rate of production and responsiveness to shifting company needs.
- Capability to manufacture medium-sized volumes of similar goods.
- Ability to rapidly adapt or extend the manufacturing procedure in response to demands.
- Ability to modify the product without triggering downtime.
- The ability to quickly generate a multitude of similar products and automate transitions.
- Increased productivity in environments involving tasks that are frequently performed or labour shortages.

4.4.3.3. Limitations of Flexible Automation

The major limitations of Flexible Automation are listed below:

- Designing and sustaining flexible automation is sometimes more challenging. It frequently needs trained professionals for operations and programming.
- The complex nature of flexible systems necessitates careful planning, accurate designs, and precise scheduling.
- Although flexible automation might result in long-term financial benefits, the initial expenses for installation may be higher than permanent automation.
- The flexibility comes with a cost, and organizations must measure the benefits with the initial investment.
- Production rates for certain flexible automation systems could be lower than those of fixed automation. The flexibility comes with a cost, and organizations must measure the benefits with the initial investment.
- Production rates for certain flexible automation systems could be lower than those of fixed automation.
- Flexible automation is nevertheless less adaptable than human workers, despite being made to fit a variety of activities. Still one of the planet's most adaptable and flexible species, humans can carry out a wide range of tasks and circumstances.

4.4.4. Reconfigurable Automation

Reconfigurable automation describes processes or systems that have the ability to adjust and modify their configuration while they are operating. The flexibility of these systems is designed to accommodate modifications without necessitating significant downtime or reengineering. Reconfigurable automation is an intriguing notion that crosses the divide between traditional hardware and software limits. Reconfigurable manufacturing systems (RMS) are a well-known application. They may alter their duties and talents to meet the needs of different component families. When production requirements change, RMS reconfigures itself in an efficient and economic manner.

Field-programmable gate arrays are reconfigurable computer platforms that provide software and hardware flexibility. Following construction, these platforms can be reprogrammed for specialised applications. Designers face a hurdle in ensuring the system's reconfiguration during runtime. The concept of reconfigurable automation enables dynamic system design adjustments. Six essential reconfigurable manufacturing systems qualities—modularity, integration, customized adaptability, capacity, interchangeability, and diagnosability—are present in the best reconfigurable manufacturing systems.

A typical reconfigurable manufacturing systems will possess some, but not all, of these characteristics. Reconfigurable manufacturing systems increases the speed at which manufacturing systems react to unforeseen events, like abrupt changes in market demand or unplanned equipment failure, when these traits are present. New items may be introduced into production quickly thanks to the reconfigurable manufacturing systems, which also makes it possible to modify production amounts in case they change unexpectedly. The ideal reconfigurable system is one that is both cost-effectively adaptable when needed and provides precisely the functionality and production capacity needed.

4.4.4.1. Benefits

The major benefits are as under:

Adaptability: Reconfigurable systems can respond to unforeseen circumstances, changing needs, or market demands.

Cost-effectiveness: Instead of developing new systems for each case, reconfigurable automation makes the best use of existing resources.

Reduced downtime: Prompt reconfiguration reduces production disruptions.

4.4.4.2. Effects

The major effects of reconfigurable systems are listed below:

Greater computational capacities: By blurring the borders between hardware and software, reconfigurable systems provide improved computing density inside a programmable medium.

Innovative Potential: Consider a production floor that fluidly transitions between different goods, demonstrating the revolutionary power of reconfigurable automation.

4.5. Design and Analysis of Automated Flow Lines

In order to ensure the proper completion of the process, a number of attributes need to be taken into account when designing and assessing automated flow lines. These parameters are discussed in this section.

4.5.1. Factor Associated in Designing of Automated Flow Lines

Important factors to take into account while designing automation are discussed below:

4.5.1.1. Planning products based on market

Product development professionals or teams of engineers shouldn't make the choice to create a product using automated design on an individual basis. For creating a product that is appropriate for automation-based assembly, it is essential to comprehend the overall needs, which include the company's objectives, promotional tactics, and lifecycle considerations. Market conditions have a significant effect on the choice of deciding whether or not to automate. If a company is attempting to capture market segments through the introduction of a new product, automation might not prove to be the best course of action, particularly in the lack of proof. However, automation reduces the need for humans to perform repetitive tasks-this is not feasible for items that need to be promptly enhanced to meet customer needs. Due to this, determining the expected return from the investment of spending in automation requires a thorough assessment of the projected lifespan and product volumes.

4.5.1.2. Key indicators of performance and operational metrics to make decisions

To assess automated machinery performance over period of time and establish standards, any automated manufacturing procedure must include a fundamental collection of operational parameters as well as performance indicators. Conventional metrics, such as initial returns, are not reliable indicators of a system's present condition. To aid in the optimization of the automated systems, look into integrating several of the indicators that are used in the manufacturing process. These metrics are frequently used in automation manufacturing to determine if equipment is available to be implemented or authorized for delivery, when it is performing exactly as anticipated, or when anything is not operating properly in normal operation.

4.5.1.3. Engaging designing solutions

An end-effector is a gripper attached to a robotic arm that allows it to interact with its surroundings in a way similarly to that of a robotic hand. Grippers are essential in the automobile production process due to their improve productivity with precise mechanical grips, fingers, and suction-cups. However, stated, humans are still an appropriate choice for assembling assignments that require handling substandard or damaged goods or components that would require an extended period for an automated system to assemble, despite the fact that grippers were first utilized in the automotive industry decades ago. As gripper technology advances, robotic grippers increasingly resemble human hands.

4.5.1.4. Nesting and crowding methodologies

A well-designed automated workflow requires exact control over the interactions between its parts. Parts must, at the outset, fulfil their intended function and integrate into the unit processing framework. Error threshold reduction minimises waste and operating costs. Parts are arranged by machines or labourers in a fixture called a nest during manufacture. These nests, which store parts in preset orientations, are models in three dimensions, tools, supports, or chambers. This method helps to prevent positioning errors by "crowding," or placing components against a predetermined, accurate location in space. Nesting and crowding techniques work effectively in automated systems due to the fact that they rely on consistency. These systems may be able to execute consistently if they operate within the constraints established throughout the product design, prototype development, and testing stages.

4.5.1.5. Value addition and cost of the product

It is important to have an understanding of material values and labour costs related to technology, growth, development, and production during the design process. This complete understanding will lead to the ability to calculate the entire cost of the products as well as the process of assembly as it relates to the finished product. A thorough understanding of labour and material costs can help you decide which areas to concentrate your efforts. These tasks might include research, process development, and methods or activities for material retrieval.

4.5.1.6. System adaptability

Establishing high-speed automated systems requires specialized tools, accuracy, and operational requirements. Accurate positioning control is often necessary throughout a production or assembly procedure due to high-speed automation.

Robotic processes may be slower, but they can adapt to changes in part placement or velocity. Not every workstation needs to be fully automated, even on the fastest systems. Process flexibility is increased, and technological hazards and expenditures are reduced through the efficient use of humans and intelligent machines.

4.5.1.7. Plans for complex and complicated procedures

There are a lot of unknowns and risks to consider during the process, even if automation seems like the ideal choice. Occasionally, despite careful execution, specific locations or techniques might not function as anticipated or fulfil the targeted performance benchmarks. It is therefore advisable to have an alternative strategy at all times. This backup strategy can be expanding a station to accommodate more activities, setting aside specific locations for objects to be dumped, or switching to a manual process in the meantime while any technical problems are fixed.

4.5.1.8. Acquire complete automation production systems

A successful outcome in automation design necessitates the careful consideration of numerous elements, making it a complex process. Upper management should have critical conversations, conversations, and investigations regarding everything from revenue and system flexibility to product advancement and appealing possibilities in order to ascertain when, where, and how automation could benefit the company. When a company decides to take an investment, it wants to collaborate with a design business that combines both technical proficiency and personalized relations. Our comprehensive strategy during the campaign begins with a thorough discussion to fully understand the goals, interests, and concerns.

4.5.2. Analysis of automated flow line

When performing an automated flow line analysis, there are two factors to consider. First, process technology and second is system technology. Process technology is the body of knowledge on the laws and theories governing the particular manufacturing process used in a production line.

The broad topic of process technology includes things like machining economy, chip control, machine tool modifications, appropriate tool utilization, and the metallurgy and machineability of the work component. By adhering to machining principles, many machining issues can be resolved. Every step of a technology's development takes years of study and experience.

4.5.2.1. Transfer line analysis without internal storage

It needs to establish particular assumptions about the functioning of the rotary indexing devices and the transfer line.

1. Workstations are utilized for processes such as machining, not assembly.
2. Although they may not be the same, the turnaround times at each workstation are always consistent.
3. Component transfers are synchronized.
4. Internal buffers cannot be retained.

On an automated assembly line, parts are fed into the first workstation, processed, and then transported to the next workstations at regular intervals. The duration of this period specifies the optimum length of cycle for the production process. Ideal cycle time (T_{ic}) is calculated by adding the processing time of the slowest workstation on the line to the transfer time.

$$T_{\text{ic}} = T_{pr} + T_t \quad \text{.............................. (1)}$$

T_{ic} = Ideal cycle time on the line

T_{pr}= Processing time at station

T_t = Transfer time

4.5.2.2. Transfer Line Analysis Using Storage Buffers

Workstations in an automated manufacturing line are connected together due to the fact that there is no internal storage for parts. When a single station fails, it changes the entire line, whether it occurs immediately or after only a few cycles of operation. Some workstations will be required to shut down for multiple reasons. The initial challenge is a lack of stations, which is followed by workstation restrictions. On an automated production line, "unfed" happens when a workstation is unable to complete its cycle due to a lack of available components. Breakdowns at any workstation along the line may result in downstream stations running out of parts, instantly or over a period of time. Even though breakdowns and line stoppages happen by mistake, they can still be assessed when they happen. There is a standard duration for each outage incident. Because to disruptions, the production line's average cycle time is longer than ideal cycle time.

The actual average production time

$$T_{p-average} = T_{ic} + F \times T_{downtime} \quad \text{.........................(2)}$$

F = Unplanned downtime Frequency, Line Stops per Cycle

$T_{downtime}$ = downtime per line stop, measured in minutes.

The downtime, $T_{downtime}$ refers to the time required for the service personnel to determine the problem, maintenance, and restore the drive.

$F \times T_{downtime}$ represents the average downtime per cycle.

Production rate can be calculated as the reciprocal of the actual average production time.

$$R_{prod.} = \frac{1}{T_{prod.}} \qquad \text{.................................(3)}$$

Where $R_{prod.}$ and $T_{prod.}$ is the actual average production rate (pc/min) and the actual average production time, respectively.

The ideal rate of production is determined by

$$R_{ic} = \frac{1}{T_c} \qquad \text{................................ (4)}$$

Where R_{ic} is ideal production rate (pc/min)

Production rates on automated lines need to be determined in hours. Due to an error in the automated transfer line endorsement, the machine tool designer estimates the required output rate as approximately one hundred percent efficiency. Although machine tool manufacturers might not be aware about how downtime influences production rates, it is important to keep in mind that the company that utilizes the line is accountable for every moment of the downtime. *Line efficiency* measure's reliability and uptime, rather than efficiency.

The following formula can be used to calculate the line efficiency:

$$E = \frac{T_{ic} + \mathrm{F} \times \mathrm{T}_{downtime}}{T_{p-average}}$$

4.6. Partial and full automation

4.6.1. Partial automation

The term "partial automation" describes the deliberate use of automated technology during some stages of the production processes. Using this approach, companies can increase production and efficiency by automating certain processes while keeping human oversight and control. It strikes a compromise between only partially and fully automated processes, offering an affordable option that can be customized to meet the specific requirements of a company. Partial automation involves using automated machinery and automated vehicles to do monotonous or hazardous tasks, allowing human workers to focus on more complex or creative elements of production. With this focused automation, productivity can be significantly increased without requiring an entirely new redesign of existing manufacturing procedures. Many assembly lines in the industrial sector have both automated and manual workstations. These partially automated production lines arise for two reasons: automation is gradually implemented to a humanly operated line, and certain manual operations are too expensive or difficult to be automated.

4.6.1.1. Automation is gradually implemented to a humanly operated line

If the demand for a product in a human-operated line increases, automating some or all of the workstations might increase productivity and lower labour costs. Automation progresses through almost fully automated lines, beginning with simpler processes. In the meanwhile, some of the line is automated. Some tasks that cannot be automated include work unit alignment, alterations, and fine-tuning during the assembling and processing stages. These procedures typically require specific knowledge and tact. This category contains a number of inspection techniques. Finding defects that human inspectors can notice may be challenging for automated inspection techniques.

Human inspectors are able to spot unforeseen imperfections and problems, however automated inspection techniques are restricted to recognizing certain deficiencies.

4.6.1.2. Some manual tasks are too costly or challenging to automate

When establishing a line's workstation sequencing, both automated and manual workstations are available. It may be too complex to automate assembly and processing stages that require unit alignment, alteration, or adjustment. These jobs typically require a person's unique human abilities and/or senses. This applies to a wide range of inspection methods. Sometimes faults in a product or component that are obvious to a human inspector are difficult for an automated inspection system to detect. Another concern is that, unlike human inspectors, automated inspection tools are confined to discovering the defects for which they were designed, whereas they can detect a wide range of unexpected issues and flaws.

4.6.2. Full Automation

The modern technology landscape is changing quickly, and industries are always looking for new and creative ways to improve efficiency, productivity, and performance in general.

Complete industrial automation is turning out to be the most significant of several ground-breaking inventions which are quickly transforming the industrial sector. The importance of a comprehensive automation strategy that incorporates the latest innovations like robotics, artificial intelligence (AI), machine learning (ML), and the Internet of Things (IoT) to automate and integrate every stage of the manufacturing process chain has been recognized by global forecasts. Furthermore, the remarkable journey towards increased efficiency, pace, and durability that complete industrial automation has allowed firms to undertake remains partially attributable to the substantial improvement in operational effectiveness that these companies experience when putting this approach into practice. Full industrial automation allows for a single network of data and support to exist between every device, all systems, and all relevant data at all times by using an extensive flow approach to the automation of all aspects, including maintenance and enhanced performance of the manufacturing process, inventory and logistics control, assurance of quality, assembly line activities, and supply chain management.

Businesses can now operate with a level of accuracy and efficiency that was unthinkable only a few years ago thanks to it.

4.6.2.1. The Essential Elements of Full Automation

Understanding the key elements that contribute to this manufacturing strategy's classification as an immersive transformation is critical to appreciating the revolutionary impact of total industrial automation. Following are the elements of full automation:

4.6.2.1.1. Machine learning algorithms

Machine learning approaches allow machines to examine data, identify patterns, and enhance performances over time without requiring programming skills. With these features, full automation systems for industry might improve production accuracy optimize consumption of energy, and potentially detect and resolve future issues before they can occur.

4.6.2.1.2. Internet of Things

The Internet of Things takes use of global connection and data sharing between components and networks. Organisations that include Internet of Things (IoT) sensors into their business processes now have fast access to data regarding the performance of machines, outside conditions, as well as the supply-chain operations. This data provides information that promotes quicker and more accurate choices, promotes preventive maintenance, and allows for optimal utilization of resources throughout the board.

4.6.2.1.3. Information Analysis

Fully automated manufacturing provides an enormous quantity of information that can be applied to several applications. Manufacturers can uncover areas for further optimization, gain valuable insights from the information gathered, and then take decisions based on data to enhance overall performance of the company by utilizing sophisticated analytics tools and processes.

4.6.2.2. The Advantages of Full Automation

Full industrial automation is supported by research, and producers intend to benefit many benefits from it. Let's examine a few benefits that this paradigm changes offers:

4.6.2.2.1. Enhanced Effectiveness

Full industrial automation reduces the possibility of human error, eliminates human involvement, and optimizes whole processes, allowing businesses to run more effectively than they have in the past. Organizations may benefit from reduced production cycles, more efficient utilisation of resources, and improved quality of goods due to automation.

4.6.2.2.2. Lowering of Expenses

Automating procedures that have previously been performed by human operators significantly saves labour costs, revision, and total utilisation of resources. At the exact time, predictive maintenance abilities serve make sure all of the equipment remains operational by identifying and resolving errors prior to they're turned into a problem, minimizing service expenses, minimising delay, and eliminating human involvement.

4.6.2.2.3. Increased safety

Human workers are mainly protected from many possibly hazardous jobs carried out by automated equipment. Full automation keeps employees out of the riskiest situations, preventing accidents and encouraging employees to work in the safest environments.

4.6.2.2.4. Flexible and Durability

Furthermore, full automation provides high production flexibility and adaptability. Manufacturers have a considerable competitive advantage due to their capacity to react rapidly and effectively to shifts in consumer preferences, modify the pace of production, and launch fresh lines of products. These skills allow them to make substantial operational modifications while minimizing disturbance.

4.6.2.2.5. Enhanced Quality Assurance

Automation systems use advanced algorithms to reduce unpredictability and problems in manufacturing processes, ensuring constant product quality. The producer can identify deviations in manufacturing parameters in real-time, take appropriate remedial action, and guarantee product quality prior to shipment by utilizing advanced sensors and artificial intelligence algorithms. Better product quality and, consequently, higher consumer happiness are the outcomes of this approach.

4.6.2.2.6. Increased Output

Full automation allows organizations to increase production rates and output volume. Production constraints are eliminated, and methods are enhanced, revised, and transformed to improve the overall process. As a result, non-value-added but essential activities are minimized, productivity improves, downtime is reduced, and customer requirements are satisfied more effectively.

4.6.2.2.7. Data-focused decision-making

Manufacturers now have incredible utilization of manufacturing data as data analysis has become increasingly integrated into full automation. Manufacturers can enhance operational performance by optimising resources, gaining valuable insights into areas for improvement, and making better choices through the analysis of such data.

4.6.2.2.8. An advantage over competitors

Manufacturers can obtain a significant competitive edge in the market by adopting full automation. For a lower price, companies are able to create more consistently high-quality products. Full automation enhances productivity and adaptability, facilitating faster manufacturing operations to customer timelines for delivery.

4.7 Automation Strategies for the Improvement of automation and production systems

4.7.1. Operational specialisation

Using specific equipment to maximise efficiency during a single task is the first technique. The concept of labour specialisation, which is employed to boost labour production, is comparable to this.

4.7.2. Integrated operations

A sequence of operations is involved in production. Numerous processing stages, possibly even hundreds, may be required for complex parts. Reducing the number of independent manufacturing machines or workstations that the part must pass through is the approach of combined operations. This is accomplished by doing many tasks on a single system, hence lowering the need for multiple independent machines. Since every system needs to be configured, this method often reduces setup time.

4.7.3. Parallel processes

Conducting the combined activities at the same workstation is a logical extension of the combined operations approach. By effectively performing two or more processing tasks simultaneously on a single workpiece, processing time is reduced overall.

4.7.4. The blending of operations

An alternative would be to incorporate numerous workstations into a single mechanism and use automated work handling devices to move parts between the stations. As a result, fewer machines are needed to schedule the product. Multiple workstations allow for the simultaneous processing of multiple parts, increasing the system's overall output.

4.7.5. Greater adaptability

By utilising the same equipment for a range of parts or products, this strategy seeks to maximise equipment utilisation in job shops and medium volume applications. It calls for the application of adaptable automation concepts. Reducing the production unit's setup and programming time is the main objective. Shorter production lead times and less work-in-process are the usual results of this.

4.7.6. Improved storage and handling of materials.

Using automated solutions for material handling and storage is a great way to cut down on idle time. Reduced work-in-process and shorter production lead times are typical benefits.

4.7.7. Online examination

Inspections for quality control are often conducted after the procedure is finished. This implies that by the time low-quality products are evaluated, they have already been produced. Corrections can be made during production by integrating inspection into the manufacturing process. Cutting down on scrap enhances product quality and complies with designer specifications.

4.7.8. Process Management and Enhancement

This integrates a number of control strategies to maximise equipment efficiency and process performance. This technique enhances product quality while cutting down on individual process durations.

4.7.9. Control of plant operations

While the prior strategy concentrated on individual manufacturing processes, this one concentrates on plant-level control. The objective is to improve management and coordination in order to maximise plant operations. Usually, a significant degree of computer networking within the production is needed for its execution.

4.7.10. Manufacturing Integrated with Computers (CIM)

By integrating industrial operations, engineering design, and business processes, we advance the previous approach. It is a device that converts a command signal from a controller into a modification of a physical parameter. Pneumatic, hydraulic, and electrical amplifiers represent the types that are needed to support controller commands.

UNIT SUMMARY

This unit describes the lean manufacturing, analysis of transfer lines, automated flow lines and brief about partial and full automation.

Solved Examples

1. What are the seven wastes in Lean?

Ans1. The seven wastes in Lean are:

- Transportation
- Inventory
- Motion
- Waiting
- Overproduction
- Overprocessing
- Defects

2. What other contexts may lean principles be applied to outside manufacturing?

Ans2. Lean principles are listed below:

- Healthcare: Shorten wait times and streamline patient care.
- Software Development: Shorten lead times and strengthen collaboration.
- Supply Chain Management: Reduce inventory and enhance logistics.
- Financial Services: Simplify processes and improve client support.

- ❖ Education: Enhance learning opportunities and administrative procedures.
- ❖ Construction: Minimal waste and effective project management.
- ❖ Retail: Increase customer satisfaction and inventory efficiency.
- ❖ Government Services: Enhance citizen services and cut down on red tape.
- ❖ Telecommunications: To minimize downtime, optimize network operations.

3. Describe the meaning of Heijunka in relation to lean manufacturing.

Ans3. A production smoothing method called heijunka aims to level out the schedule, reducing anomalies and facilitating a more predictable workflow. The term "heijunka" in lean manufacturing refers to smoothing or levelling production. It involves evenly distributing and balancing the production effort over time as opposed to seeing significant fluctuations. Reducing inventory, minimizing overproduction, and delivering a more reliable and effective production flow are the objectives. Heijunka guarantees a steady production rate, which helps businesses adapt more skilfully to changes in customer demand.

4. What role does Total Productive Maintenance (TPM) play in the Lean methodology?

Ans4. Proactive equipment maintenance is heavily emphasized in TPM in Lean to reduce unanticipated downtime, increase equipment effectiveness, and anticipate issues. Total Productive Maintenance (TPM) is an essential part of Lean manufacturing since its goal is to reduce downtime and boost equipment performance. It aims for a zero percent failure, defect, and accident rate. By integrating preventative maintenance, self-governing maintenance, and continuous improvement in accordance with the principles of lean manufacturing, TPM improves overall equipment performance and aids in the reduction of waste in industrial operations.

Exercises

Q1. What do you mean by lean manufacturing? Explain briefly.

Q2. Differentiate between fixed and flexible automation?

Q3. Explain briefly programmable and reconfigurable factory automation.

Q4. Explain in brief design and analysis of automated flow lines.

Q5. What is the difference between partial and full automation?

Q6. How can we perform analysis of transfer lines without storage?

Q7. How can we perform analysis of transfer lines with storage?

Q8. Explain production rate and line efficiency in automated flow lines.

Multiple Choice Questions

1. Which of the following is not an example of automation?
   a. Fixed
   b. Flexible
   c. Numerical
   d. Programmable

2. Which types of production processes are most suited to fixed automation?
   a. Mass
   b. Batch
   c. Customized
   d. Job-based

3. Which of the following is not a characteristic of programmable automation?
   a. Lower production rates compared to fixed automation
   b. Limited flexibility for product design variations
   c. Programmability
   d. Uses general purpose equipment

4. Which industries can benefit from programmable automation?
   a. Batch
   b. Food processing
   c. Job
   d. Mass production

5. Which form of automation should an industry that manufactures automotive bearings implement?
   a. Programmable
   b. Flexible
   c. Fixed
   d. No automation

6. Which of the following are characteristics of flexible automation?
   a. Unable to handle variations in product configuration
   b. Requires Numerical Control machine tools
   c. Similar to fixed automation
   d. Provides flexibility for product design

7. Which of the following represents the lowest level of the automation hierarchy?
   a. Machine level
   b. Device level
   c. Plant level
   d. Cell level

8. Which level of automation does a powered conveyor represent?
   a. Plant level
   b. Enterprise level 1
   c. Device level
   d. Machine level

9. Which of the following represents the highest level of automation?
   a. Device level
   b. Plant level
   c. Machine level
   d. Enterprise level

10. Cell/system-level automation includes services such as process planning, shop floor control, and quality control.
   a. False
   b. True

11. A manufacturing cell is made up of actuators, sensors, and other hardware components.
   a. False
   b. True

12. ____ is a production strategy in which distinct items are produced in a small batch or group based on commonalities.
   a. Production technology
   b. Group technology

c. Flexible manufacturing systems

d. none of the above

13. What is another name for automation testing?

a. Test Design

b. Test Process

c. Automated Testing

d. Test Automation

14. Which of the following tests cannot be automated?

a. Unit testing

b. Regression testing

c. Exploratory testing

d. End-to-end testing

15. What is the abbreviation for PID in programmable controllers?

a. Productive integral

b. Proportional integral

c. Productive integral device

d. Proportional intellectual device

16. Personal computers can easily link to the process control equipment.

a. True

b. False

17. Which function performs addition, subtraction, and multiplication?

a. Binomial Distribution

b. Arithmetic Functions

c. Probability Functions

d. Complex Integral Functions

18. Which of the following functions can conduct matrix operations?

a. Matrix

b. Arithmetic

c. Complex

d. Binomial

19. What is a transfer line?
    a. A line linking two separate towns
    b. A beamline transporting particles between accelerator components
    c. An international phone line
    d. A conveyor belt at a factory

20. Which control provides the same function as the machine control unit?
    a. Cellular control
    b. Functional and productive control
    c. Protocol control
    d. Motion and servomotor control

Answers for multiple choice questions:

Keys for multiple choice questions: 1(c), 2(a), 3(a), 4(a), 5(a), 6(d), 7(b), 8(d), 9(a), 10(b), 11(a), 12(b), 13(d), 14(c), 15(c), 16(a), 17(b), 18(a), 19(b), 20(d)

KNOW MORE

For more information related to this topic scan the QR code,

OR

Type this link in your browser

https://ufile.io/7oix0qvt

References

1. https://onlinecourses.nptel.ac.in/noc22_me50/preview
2. Mikell P. Groover, Automation, Production Systems and Computer Integrated Manufacturing, Fourth Edition, Pearson. USA (2015).
3. https://mrcet.com/downloads/digital_notes/ME/IV%20year/AIM%20all%20units_3122018.pdf
4. https://www.svsulibrary.in/faculty_Notes/Unit-%20Automated%20flow%20lines.pdf

5 Automation Tools and Techniques

UNIT SPECIFICS

Automation technologies and techniques play a vital part in automation firms. This chapter describes many types of automation technologies and procedures used by most industries.

RATIONALE

Knowledge of automation tools and methods is necessary, as is the ability to recognize sectors where full automation is prevalent.

PRE-REQUISITE

Knowledge of automation tools and techniques

UNIT OUTCOMES

List of outcomes of this unit is as follows:

U5-O1: Students should be able to understand mechanical, electro-mechanical, pneumatic and hydraulic systems

U5-O2: Students should be able to know about process monitoring, data analysis and control using actuators and robots

U5-O3: Should be able to understand automatic guided vehicles, automated inspection and measurement, Machine vision, AI and machine learning

Unit Outcomes	Expected Mapping with Programme Outcomes *(1- Weak Correlation; 2- Medium correlation; 3- Strong Correlation)*					
	PO-1	PO-2	PO-3	PO-4	PO-5	PO-6
U5-O1	3	1	3	1	1	2
U5-O2	3	3	2	2	2	3
U5-O3	3	3	1	2	1	3

An introduction of the mechanical, electro-mechanical, pneumatic, and hydraulic systems is provided, along with a detailed discussion of data analysis, process monitoring, actuator control, and sensor integration. Automatic guided vehicles, automated measurement and inspection, including CMM and 3D scanning, are defined in this chapter. This chapter provides more information on machine learning, artificial intelligence, and vision.

5.1. Mechanical System

Physical parts such as shafts, gears, chains, and belts are used in mechanical systems to transmit power. To achieve their objectives, these systems rely on mechanical motion.

5.1.1. Shafts

A shaft is a rotating machine part with a circular cross section that is used to transfer power between different parts of the machine or from a generator to an absorber. Shafts perform an important function in machinery. They sustain rotating parts like pulleys and gears, which are supported by rigid machine casing-mounted bearings. Power must be transferred from one rotating component to another that is attached to or supported by the shafts. They consequently feel bending moment from the responses of the elements they support and torque from power transfer. Axles, which support spinning components but do not transmit power, are not the same as shafts. Shafts can be solid or hollow, and their cross sections are always round. There are four types of shafts: articulated, flexible, cranked, and straight. Power transmission is most frequently accomplished with straight shafts.

5.1.1.2. Shaft Types

Shafts can be broadly divided into two categories:

5.1.1.2.1. Transmission shafts: Power is transferred between the power source and the machine that absorbs it using gearbox shafts. for instance, all factory shafts, line shafts and countershafts.

5.1.1.2.2. Machine shafts: Shafts used in machines are an essential component of the machine. for instance, the crankshaft

5.1.1.2.3. Axle shafts: In vehicles, axle shafts are used.

5.1.1.2.4. Spindle shaft: A revolving shaft fitted with a fixture to hold a tool or workpiece is called a spindle shaft.

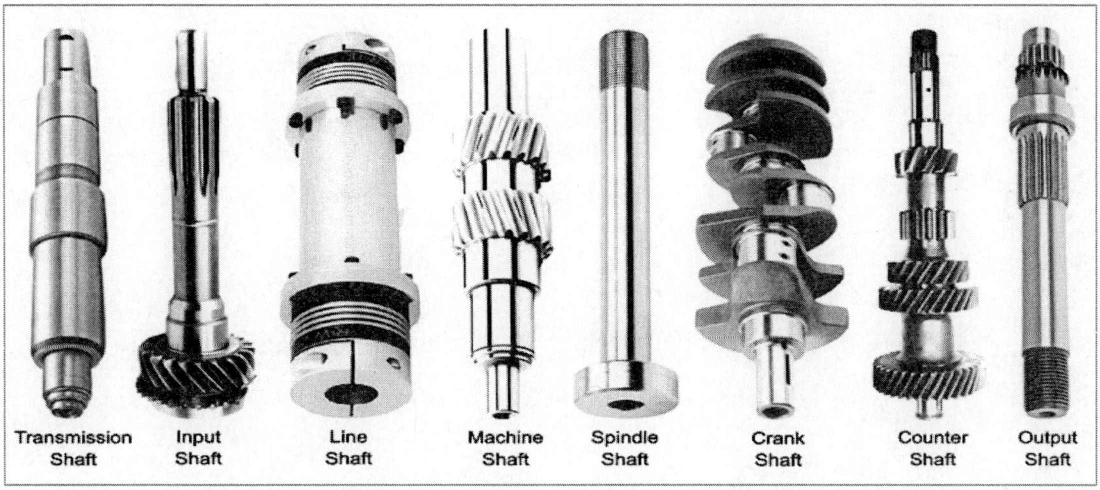

Fig. 5.1. Different types of Shafts

5.1.2. Gears

A gear, as the name suggests, is a rotating circular machine component that transfers torque by meshing with another toothed component. In the case of a gearwheel, the teeth are inserted and called cogs. Another typical term for a gear is a cog. Due to their teeth, gears have the advantage of not slipping. An enormously valuable gearbox system for rotating on different axes is made up of a series of gears. A shaft's output speed can be managed with the help of gears. Through the use of a gear arrangement, the output shaft can rotate at half the engine speed, increasing torque while decreasing speed. In high-load environments, gears are frequently used to provide more precise and noticeable control over a shaft's movement. This is one advantage that gears possess over conventional pulley systems. A gear is a kind of machine component that has uniformly spaced teeth surrounding its conical or cylindrical surfaces.

The history of gears is long, dating back to the works of Archimedes in the first century B.C. in ancient Greece. There are many different types of gears such as: Spur Gear, Helical Gear, Gear Rack, Bevel Gear, Spiral Bevel Gear, Screw Gear, Double Helical Gear, Herringbone Gear, Hypoid Gear, Miter Gear, Worm Gear, Internal gear.

Fig. 5.2. Different types of Gears

The diameters of the two pulleys can be adjusted to control the speed of the driven shaft. The amount of electricity transmitted relies on the following criteria.

1. The speed of the belt.
2. The tension at which the belt fits on pulleys.
3. The area where contact occurs between the belt and the smaller pulley.

Belt drives are among the most often utilized methods for transmitting power or rotary motion between two parallel shafts.

Types of Belt drive:

(a) Open belt drive

(b) Cross belt drive

(c) Quarter turn belt drive

(d) Belt drive with idler pulleys

(e) Fast and loose pulley drive

(f) Cone pulley drive

(g) Compound belt drive

(a) Open belt drive

Shafts that are parallel and rotate in a single direction are used in an open belts drive. The driver then shifts the belt to the second side by pulling it from the first. The lower side belt will therefore be tighter than the top side belt. The term "tight side belt" refers to the lower side belt, while "slack side belt" refers to the top side belt. The belt should be tight at the bottom and loose at the top when the shafts are too far apart. This happens so that the load encourages the top side to relax and becoming less vibrant, increasing the degree of contact.

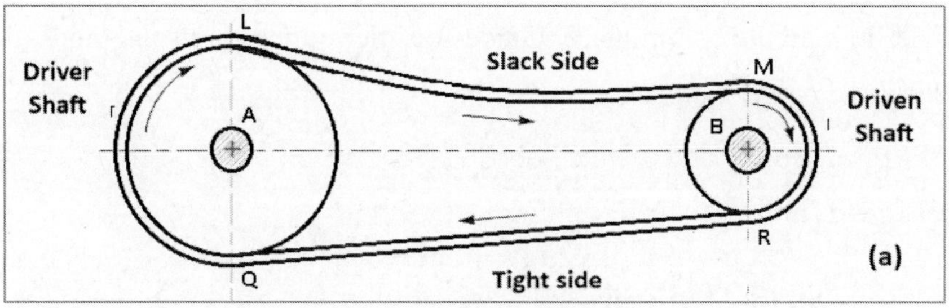

Fig. 5.3. (a) Open belt drive

(b) Cross belt drive

Rotating shafts are used in cross or twisted belt drives, which can be oriented either parallel or opposite. Here, the driver takes the belt off of one side and puts it on the other. Consequently, there will be more stress on the bottom side of the belt than the top. The term "tight side" refers to the belt with high tension and "loose side" to the belt with low tension. With this type of belt drive, two parallel shafts rotate in the opposing direction around a belt. The belt wears away at the crossroads from scraping against itself.

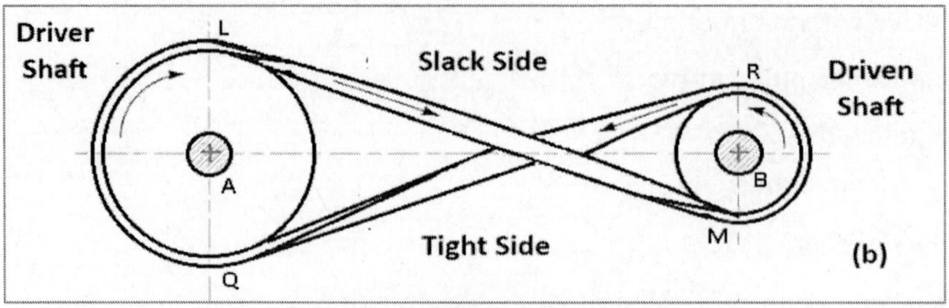

Fig. 5.3. (b) Cross belt drive

(c) Quarter turn belt drive

The majority of belt drives are limited to using parallel shafts. That might not always be the case, though. When spinning shafts are at the correct angles, belt drives with a quarter turn can be employed. After a quarter turn, the belt in a quarter turn belt drive wraps around two perpendicular shafts. The pulley needs to be at least 40% wider than the cross-section of the belt in order to hold the belt in place. Guides or idler pulleys are sometimes used to enhance belt tracking and prevent slippage.

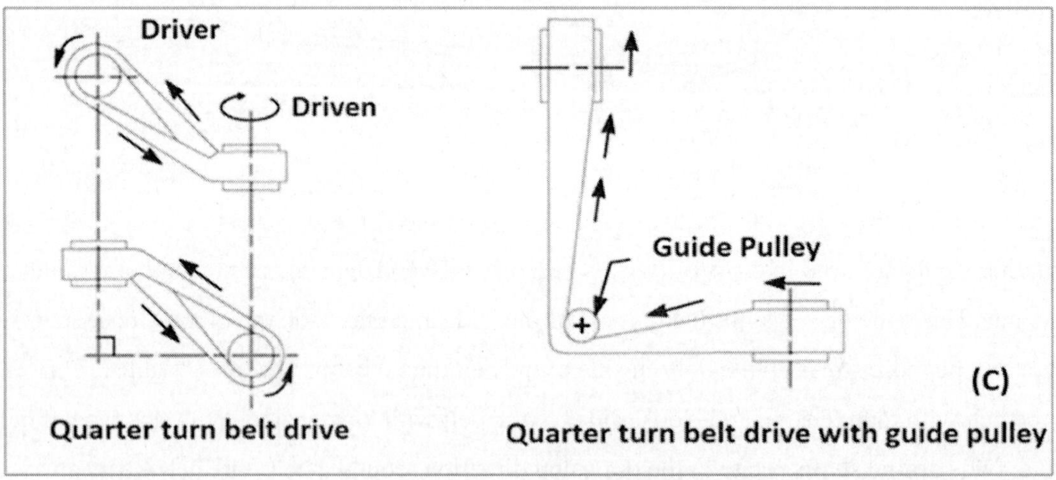

Fig. 5.3. (c) Quarter turn belt drive

d) Belt drives with idler pulleys

When shafts are aligned parallel and an open belt cannot be used due to a short angle of contact on the shorter pulley, an idler pulley belt mechanism is utilized. By minimizing belt vibrations and raising the wrapping angle of a belt on the working pulleys, idler pulleys can enhance belt drive performance. Automobile engines utilize idler pulleys to provide a positive clutching action. The speed of the belt and its output speed remain unchanged when an idler pulley is resized.

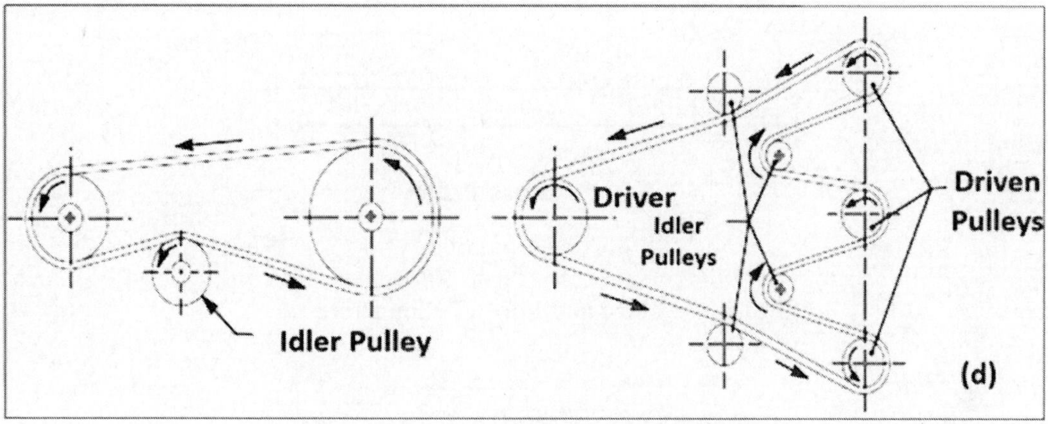

Fig. 5.3. (d) Belt drives with idler pulleys

(e) Fast and Loose Pulley Drive

When the driven or machine shaft can be starting or ended at any time without affecting the driving shaft, and such type of belt-driven system is used. A fast pulley is one that rotates at the same speed as the machine shaft and is attached to it. A loose pulley cannot transfer any power; it can only travel freely across the machine shaft. A sliding bar with belt forks is used to press the belt onto the loose pulley in order to stop the driven shaft. The belt can run loosely on the loose pulley since its rim is larger than the quick pulley's. In order to reduce wear and friction, loose pulleys usually have longer hubs, and they need to be properly lubricated.

To stop axial movement, the free pulley has a cast iron or gun-metal bushing with a collar at one end.

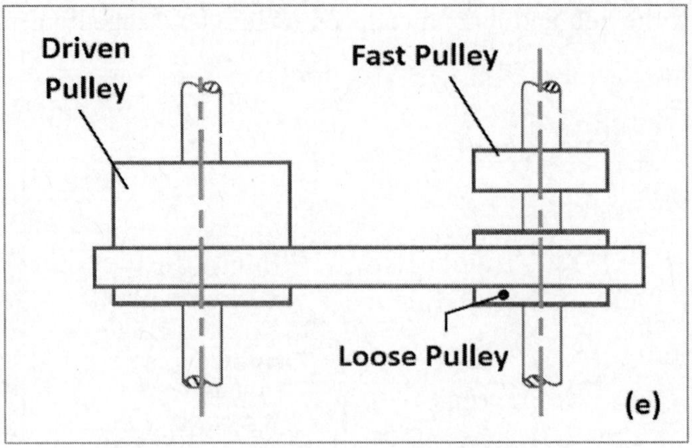

Fig. 5.3. (e) Fast and Loose Pulley Drive

(f) Cone pulley drive

The driven pulley in this particular type of belt drive has several dimensions. The pulley is called a stepped cone pulley drive due to its stepped cone-like appearance. When the shaft that is being driven needs to rotate at various rates, this drive is deployed. By changing the belt to a smaller or greater size stepping on the pulley, the driven shaft's velocity can be adjusted. Machines for drilling and turning centers are common devices that use this kind of motor. Using a stepped cone pulley, one can get varying output speeds with the same driving motor.

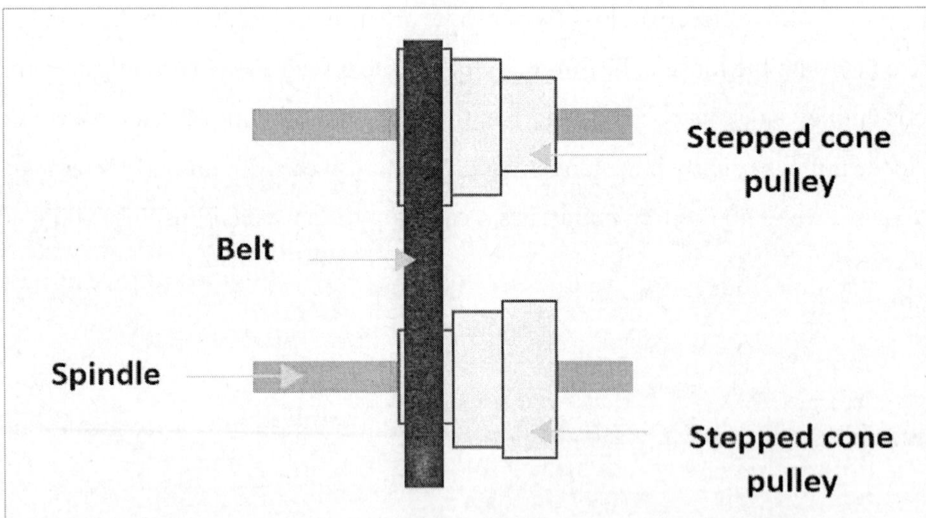

Fig. 5.3. (f) Cone pulley drive

(g) Compound belt drive

Belt drives are frequently used to lower shaft speed. The majority of belt drives transfer motion from a smaller to a larger pulley for this reason, among others. On the other hand, the speed ratio that can be achieved with just one set of pulleys might not always be sufficient. Compound belt drives can be used by designers in these situations to attain greater speed ratios. More than two shafts make up a compound belt drive, and each shaft has multiple pulleys keyed to at least one of them. The driving pulley uses several shafts to transfer power from one shaft to another. With this configuration, the speed ratio is increased without requiring a larger driven pulley or a lot more space.

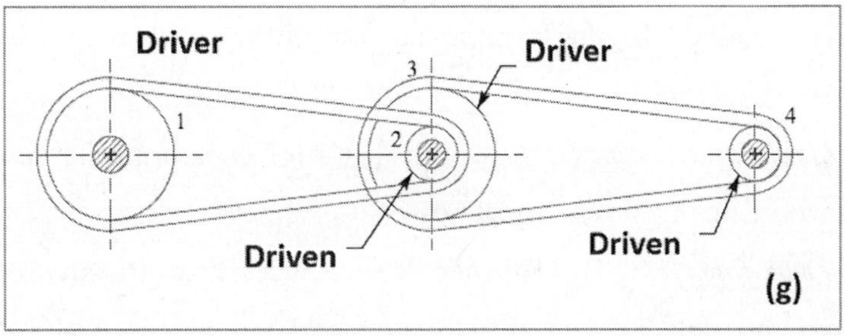

Fig. 5.3. (g) Compound belt drive

5.2. Electro-mechanical

Electromechanical systems include approaches and processes from both electrical and mechanical engineering. These systems investigate the interaction of electrical and mechanical components, intended to figure out how they work together. The combination of mechanical and electrical engineering is known as electromechanics. It focuses on how electrical and mechanical systems interact in their whole as well as with each other. A specific type of electromechanical system that combines electronic and mechanical components into one unit is called an electromechanical unit.

These assemblies fall into two categories: subgroups, that are made up of the whole system units, sometimes known as box assemblies, and frame connectivity, that consists of board-level links. The study of the interaction between electrical and mechanical systems is called electromechanics. It includes devices like motors that convert electrical energy to mechanical motion and generators that do the reverse. Understanding electromechanical assemblies in all of its forms and applications is vital due to the fact that they can be as simple as they are highly complex. Our knowledgeable staff has put together comprehensive information about electromechanical assemblies, outlining what they are, the types that are readily accessible, and the sectors and uses in which they are implemented.

Various industries and applications, such as the medical, environmentally friendly technology, commercial, a computer system, security forces, interactions, shipping, testing and instruments, and communications via satellite, heavily rely on electromechanical assembly. The range of such uses highlights the significance of electromechanical assemblies in the advancement of technology and the requirement for dependable manufacturing and design capabilities to ensure peak performance. Electromechanical assemblies are designed with a particular objective in mind. Regularly manufactured electromechanical assemblies include the following:

Assembly of the Cable and Harness: Assembly parts for cables and harnesses are wires or cables used to transport signals or electrical power.

Assemblies for Transformers: Transformers are devices that transfer electrical energy between two or more circuits. They modify the voltage level in accordance with the needs of the application.

Assembly of the Power Supply: Power supplies generate electricity for at least one electric load by converting current to the appropriate voltage and format. It is feasible to build an independent power supply or integrate appliances.

DIN Rail Assemblies: DIN rails, sometimes referred to as mounting rails, are used to mount additional components in electromechanical assemblies. They have to be assembled in line with the components and subassemblies.

Panel Assemblies: A few electromechanical assemblies on panels regulate the distribution of electricity among linked circuits.

Switch and Sensor Assemblies: Essential parts of electrical systems are switch and sensor assemblies. Switch assemblies are typically used to connect or disconnect electrical parts from a power source, whereas sensor assemblies convert electrical impulses from outside forces like movement, light, warmth, or sounds.

Parts utilized in Electromechanical Systems

Electromechanical assemblies come in many different varieties such as:

Solenoids: Solenoids are electromechanical devices that operate a valve or plunger by using a magnetic field. In the automotive, industrial, and medical fields, they are frequently used.

***Actuators**:* Actuators are mechanical motion-producing devices that run on electrical energy. They can be applied to the relocation of switches, valves, and other mechanical parts.

Motors: Motors are machines that rotate by utilizing electrical energy. They are employed in many different fields, including as robotics, transportation, and manufacturing.

Sensors: Sensors are machines that identify changes in their surroundings and convert them into electrical impulses. Numerous other factors, including location, pressure, and temperature, can be ascertained using them.

Generators: Machines called generators convert mechanical energy into electrical energy. In addition to being utilized in backup and renewable energy systems, they also produce electricity.

Transformers: Transformers are devices that transfer electrical energy between circuits via the use of magnetic induction. They are employed in power distribution networks to raise or lower voltage levels.

Actuated valves: These are hydraulic, pneumatic, or electric valves that are managed by an actuator. They are used in many different industrial processes, including as purification of water, extraction of oil and gas, and processing of chemicals.

5.3. Pneumatic

Pneumatics is a subject of engineering that uses airflow or high-pressure air to complete specific tasks. A pneumatic system consists of components that transform compressed air pressure energy into mechanical work. Pneumatic technologies are employed when human strength and precision are insufficient. Pneumatic systems are now commonly employed to automate a variety of functions across industries.

To accomplish productive labour, a pneumatic system transfers energy from a power-generating source to a power-consuming point by employing compressed gas, usually air, as a fluid. The image shows a basic pneumatic system design made up of fundamental parts.

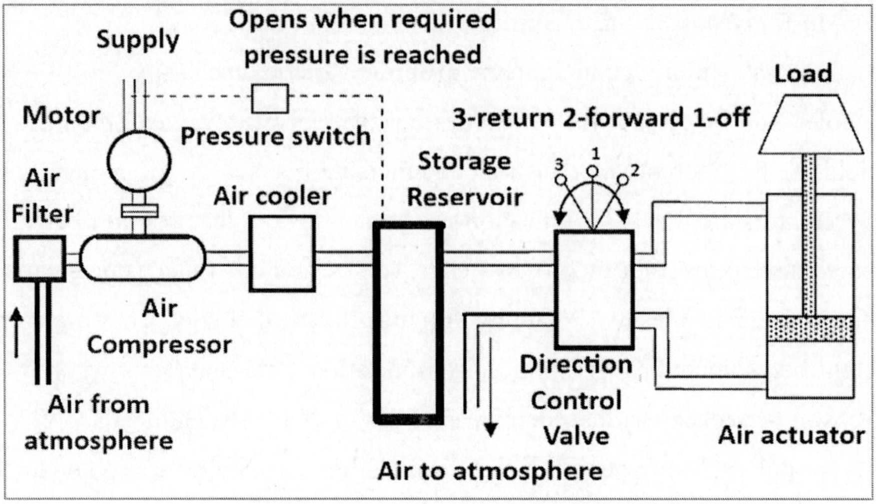

Fig. 5.4. Basic Components of Pneumatic System

5.4. Hydraulic System

In hydraulic power generator units, compressed liquid is employed as a fluid to transfer power from a power-generating source to a power-consuming location for productive labour. The figure illustrates a basic hydraulic system network made up of basic components. In hydraulic systems, hydraulic fluid is used as a medium for transfer of power. The hydraulic system operates on the basis of Pascal's law, that states that "pressure in a liquid at rest is transmitted equally in all directions". The fluid medium employed is hydraulic fluid, that can be either water, mineral oil, or a combination of both.

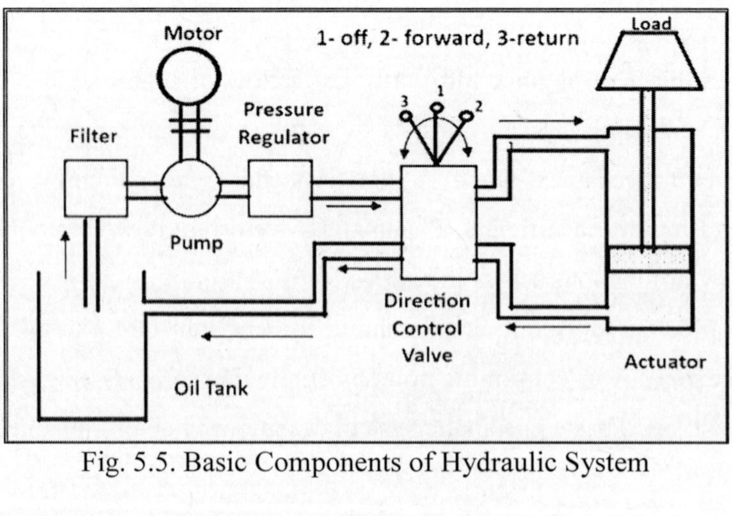

Fig. 5.5. Basic Components of Hydraulic System

5.4.1. Basic Components of Hydraulic System

5.4.1.1. Actuator

It is a device that uses fluid power to generate mechanical power for practical purposes. Actuators can provide linear or rotating motion, such as hydraulic cylinders or motors. The hydraulic pump circulates pressurized hydraulic fluid to the actuators, which convert the fluid's energy into mechanical energy. This mechanical energy is utilized to perform the task.

Actuator Types

1. Linear actuator.
2. Rotary actuators.

There are two types of rotary actuators: continuous and semi-rotary.

5.4.1.2. Pump

It converts mechanical energy into hydraulic energy and uses it to force fluid from the reservoir to the rest of the hydraulic system. A pump, which is the core of a hydraulic system, turns

mechanical energy into hydraulic power. The mechanical energy is given to the pump using a prime mover, such as an electric motor. The pump's mechanical motion creates a partial vacuum at the inlet. This allows air pressure to push fluid through the inlet line and into the pump. The pump subsequently transports the fluid into the hydraulic system.

Significance of pump

- They change mechanical energy into hydraulic energy
- The volumetric efficiency of the pump is quite high
- They offer high-performance qualities under various speeds and pressures
- Pumps used to provide high pressure in the hydraulic system

5.4.1.3. Valves

Valves regulate the flow rate, pressure, and direction of a fluid as it moves through an interconnected system. A directional control valve. Pump Oil tank Filter Actuator A pressure regulator. A fluid power system can be separated into three sections. The pump and prime mover make up the power input component. The control segment consists of valves that control the direction, pressure, and flow rate. The power output section consists of actuators and a load. This unit is intended for the following types of control valves.

- ❖ Directional control valves
- ❖ Pressure control valves
- ❖ Flow control valves

Directional Control Valves

Direction control valves regulate the flow direction in a circuit, which can, among other things, control the actuator's direction. Pressure control valves regulate the pressure level, which influences the output force of a cylinder or the torque of a motor. Flow control valves regulate the flow rate of the fluid, hence controlling the speed of the actuators.

5.4.1.3.1. Various valve types and their purposes

- ❖ *Pressure relief valves:* When the pressure surpasses the predetermined point, the relief valve opens and bypasses the fluid. These are utilized in almost all circuits.
- ❖ *Pressure reducing valves:* This valve is used to keep hydraulic systems' pressures low in specific regions.
- ❖ *Unloading valves:* Punching presses use high-low pump circuits, in which two pumps move an actuator at high speed but low pressure.
- ❖ *Counterbalance valves:* They stop an overly rapid acceleration of a load. When a weight is the load in a vertical cylinder, this can occur. At the end of its journey, if the load is stopped suddenly, it could damage both the load and the cylinder.
- ❖ *External power source:* A motor is required to drive the pump. Without external power source pump cannot works.
- ❖ *Oil Tank or Reservoir:* Hydraulic oil is kept in this oil storage tank. After serving a useful purpose in an actuator, the oil is routed with a number of tubes before being put back into the oil tank. Oil warmers are attached to air tanks in cold climates. Hydraulic fluids, most often hydraulic oil, are kept in reservoirs.
- ❖ *Pipelines:* The functional link for oil flow in a hydraulic system is called a pipeline. The physical properties of pipe systems have a big impact on oil flow efficiency. There are two types of pipes: Oil pipelines under pressure and oil transport pipes for low pressure or abandoned oil. Hose, pipes, and fittings make form a fluid powered pipeline.
- ❖ *Filters:* It removes undesirable particles from the fluid system, keeping it clean and efficient while preventing damage to the actuator and valves.

When hydraulic fluids get contaminated, hydraulic systems can clog and malfunction as a result of internal wear. They require filtering to remove contaminants.

Filters are classified as:

- Reservoir filters
- Line Filters
- Filters that operate offline
- Improved cleaning tools

Regulator of pressure: The necessary hydraulic fluid pressure is managed by the pressure regulator. The closed-loop form of piping shown in the image transports fluid from the storage tank to one side of the piston and back to the tank on the other. Fluid is drawn from the tank by a pump, which creates fluid flow at the required pressure. The extra fluid returns to the reservoir and remains there until the requisite amount of pressure is reached if the fluid pressure is higher than what is necessary.

Accumulators: Hydraulic fluid is stored under pressure in accumulators. One way to conserve energy for later use is to retain hydraulic fluid under pressure. In a hydraulic system, the most common application for an accumulator is probably to augment pump flow when a high flow rate is needed for a brief duration. There are various kinds of accumulators, one of which is weight-loaded. There are various types of accumulators such as gas-charged, spring-loaded, piston, bladder, and diaphragm type.

Hydraulic Power Pack: The energy required for the hydraulic installation is provided by the hydraulic power unit. The reservoir, drive, hydraulic pump, filter, cooler, and pressure release valve are the main parts of power packs. Pumps and motor units can be mounted on tanks or placed independently, and packs are frequently offered in both vertical and horizontal configurations. With the right control valve, the basic unit can be connected to the cylinders or actuators. The hydraulic fluid, which acts as the working medium, is stored in a reservoir or tank that makes up the hydraulic power packs.

5.5. Sensors Integration:

Sensor integration is an essential component of automation and control systems that raises accuracy, dependability, and productivity. Analogous to sensor fusion, sensor integration comprises integrating information from multiple sensors in order to model an actual environment or generate artificial intelligence for more precise and consistent events management. The goal of sensor fusion is to increase control system intelligence or replicate real-world environments. It requires gathering data from a variety of sensors in order to provide reliable management despite faulty input and environmental changes. The integration of sensors into intelligent devices and systems has enhanced the capacity to track, evaluate, and

compile data at the local level. Networked and autonomous sensors sample and quantify a range of physical characteristics. Raw data collection, processing, and transmission over network connections are made possible by the development of smart sensors, which is made possible by wireless and fixed-access networks.

Advantages of Sensors Integration:

Following are the advantages of sensor's integration:

Automation: To automate tasks and procedures, automation significantly depends on sensors. By recognizing particular physical characteristics, they may automate tasks, increasing accuracy and efficiency across a range of sectors.

Real-Time Data: Real-time data gathering and monitoring are made possible by sensors. This ability facilitates quick and well-informed decision-making. Vital information about the state of the environment, automobile performance, and industrial processes can be obtained from sensors.

5.6. Process monitoring

Process monitoring is the continuous monitoring and evaluation of how processes work to gauge effectiveness, spot problems, and pinpoint areas in need of development. The core, assistance, and long-tail operational procedures must all operate smoothly and dependably, and this requires the surveillance of application-related functions. Regular process monitoring can help to cut down on wastage and detect issues prior to they affect your company. The Food and Drug Administration is in charge of ensuring the safety, quality, and effectiveness of biological commodities, healthcare equipment, vaccines, and medications for humans and animals. Regarding automation in the medical field, there are a number of things to take into account.

5.7. Data analysis and control

Control data analysis can refer to two different concepts: Control data is sometimes known as external data or third-party data. By combining control data into a model, data scientists can find external variables that have influenced previous outcomes, develop linkages between these aspects, and predict future company outcomes based on the same external factors.

5.8. Pick and Place Robots

These days, pick-and-place robots are frequently used in manufacturing settings. Pick and place robots offer organizations to implement automated solutions for moving and positioning products. It takes little mental effort to lift and move objects; these are easy tasks. Although the workforce may be more suitable for various jobs demanding a greater cognitive potential, engaging humans for these positions may not be efficient. These repetitive tasks are handled by pick-and-place robots. In order to lift items off a moving conveyor belt, these robots are usually equipped with monitoring and vision systems. Automation for pick and place speeds up the process of gathering components or other items and arranging them in various places. Increasing manufacturing rates is a benefit of automating this operation. Robots that pick and put tasks complete laborious tasks, freeing up workers to concentrate on more complex tasks.

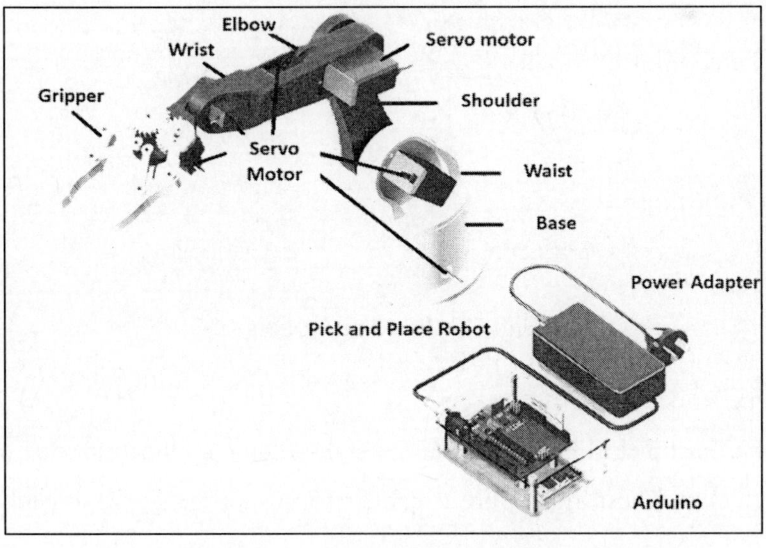

Fig. 5.6. Pick and Place Robots

5.9. Welding Robots

Robotic welding involves automated workpiece handling, wire feeding, and torch movement. The welding operator configures all of the welding features using the machine controls. Robotic welding use machinery that has welding configurations programmed into devices so that they are able to be retrieved later. Furthermore, the handling of welding components is automated, so no physical effort is required. This technique involves using a robotic arm that is fitted with welding equipment to complete welding activities. Robotics, welding, control systems, sensor technologies, and artificial intelligence are all intricately combined in this task. Robotic welding produced significantly faster, more consistent, and more accurate welds. The method may move in three dimensions and can be programmed. Robots can be programmed by welders to perform precise tasks using welding instruments and actions. Because the robot can follow instructions, welders can complete tasks more quickly than anticipated. Consequently, complicated welding processes can be completed by robots without the need for direct human involvement. Robotic welding is most commonly used to join metal parts. Schematic view of welding robot is shown in Figure 5.7.

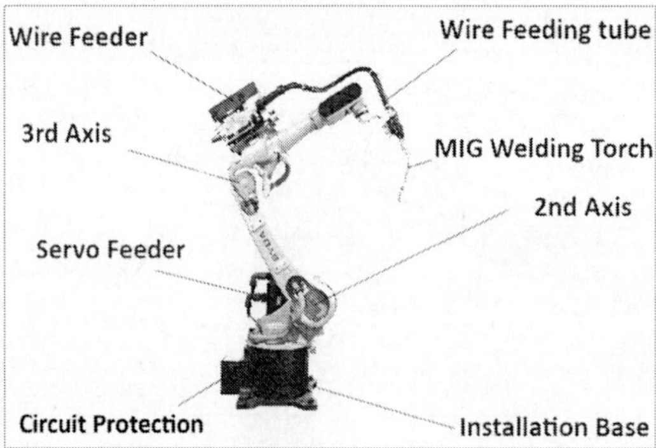

Fig. 5.7. Welding Robots

Types of Welding Robots:

Fast Pick Robots: Fast pick robots are ideal for high-volume applications due to their ability to pick items quickly. These robots are capable of transporting approximately 300 objects every hour.

Robotic Arms: Robotic arms are the most basic and frequent sort of pick and place robot. As previously stated, they are used as 5 and 6-axis robotic arms. 6-axis robotic arms operate similarly to cartesian robots but have poorer positioning precision than delta robots.

Delta Robots: Delta robots can pick and position things into specified assembly patterns or groups. These robots can be outfitted with sensors or vision systems to choose goods based on their colour or size.

Collaborative Robots: As the name suggests, collaborative robots cooperate with people. They are there to direct people to the desired or picking area. These robots are capable of planning the best route to save down on transportation time.

5.9.1. Advantages of Welding Robots

5.9.1.1. Consistent quality

Robots are not distracted. They are able to keep the weld quickly, electrical current, and several other parameters constant. They are therefore able to reliably create welds of excellent quality. Robotic welding is a good fit for tasks involving high standards of quality in welding.

5.9.1.2. Reduce consumption and waste

Robots adhere to predetermined parameters; therefore, robotic automation assures uniform quality. When under cognitive stress, human operators are more likely to make mistakes. In a highly competitive job market, a company with a high turnover rate may be forced to hire new employees who have no relevant prior experience. Novice employees are more likely to make mistakes than experienced ones. The results of automation can be quite consistent. Robots reduce scrap and rework. Reducing scrap minimizes the amount of waste that ends up in landfills.

5.10. Painting Robots

Painting Robots are becoming more prevalent in the manufacturing, building, and automobile sectors. The following are the benefits of painting robots. Painting robots apply coatings with high precision and consistency. They often work in a manufacturing environment. Paint robots have long been utilized in the automotive industry. Over the past few years, painting robots have advanced significantly. More applications have become viable. Modern painting robots feature arms with six degrees of freedom. This means that they can paint both the interior and exterior of an automobile. Robot painters can routinely approach locations that are impossible for humans to reach. Furthermore, complicated parts with angular or curved surfaces may be painted or coated.

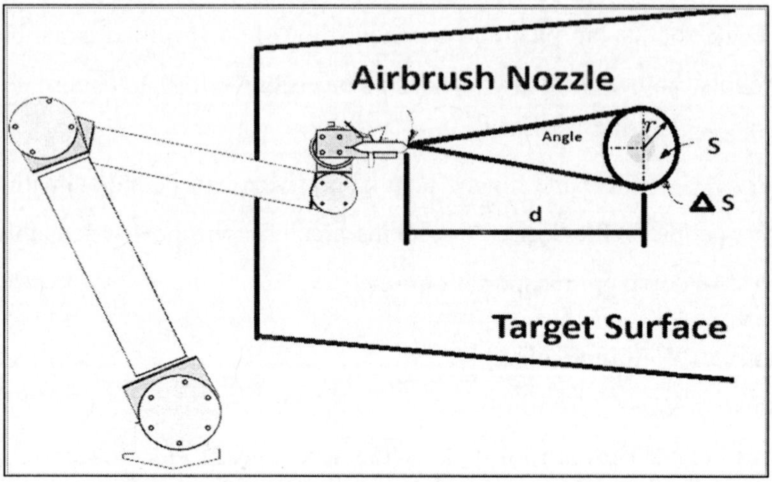

Fig. 5.8. Painting Robots

5.10.1. Benefits of Painting Robots

Employing painting robots has the following advantages:

- Since robots are significantly more adept at maintaining a steady speed than humans are, they can guarantee an even coating.
- The robotic painting arm moves incredibly precisely. Comparing the robot's position to that of a human painter, it will be far more consistent as well as precise.
- Approximately thirty times faster than manual labours.
- protecting employees from dangerous chemicals and fumes.
- decreased expenses by reducing the quantity of coating waste.

5.11. Automatic Guided Vehicles

An automatic guided vehicle system is a set of battery-operated, computer-controlled transport vehicles that can work on paved terrain such as factory or warehouse premises without the need for a driver or controller to be on board. Automated vehicles, like pallets, wagons, or containers, move items throughout manufacturing and warehousing facilities automatically and without the need for an operator.

These vehicles are called materials handling systems. These technologies improve efficiency, minimize damage to commodities, and reduce costs through minimizing the number of workers needed to finish an operation. A.M. Barrett Jr. developed the first ground-based autonomous vehicle in 1954. An overhead wire guides a modified towing truck pulling a trailer through a food warehouse. Barrett later introduced commercial AGVs.

Volvo introduced automated guided vehicles in 1973 to serve as assembly platforms for moving automobile bodies during the last stages of production. Afterwards, Volvo sold their unit load AGVs to other automakers. Automated guided vehicles are conveyors that run on their own independently without assistance from a human. They use load-bearing devices that can be either passive or active, pulling and carrying items. Automated guided vehicles (AGVs) are becoming more and more significant in today's logistics. The phrase refers to an integrated system that includes autonomous guided vehicles, loading stations, master controls, and data transmission units. Guided vehicles that are automated have several applications. The main idea is that they transfer items from the starting point A to destination B without requiring human interaction, hence replacing non-value-adding transit.

AGVs provide several advantages for standard warehouse operations, including as removing labor-intensive transport responsibilities from employees, improving process stability, and reducing the possibility of errors and mishaps in the warehouse, containers, and other items. The purpose of boat trailers is to tow boats. These trailers are chosen according to the kind and kind of boat they will tow, and they are made to be easily loaded into and unloaded from the water. They belong to a different category because they are open trailers designed with the express purpose of holding and accommodating boats.

5.11.1. Types of AGVs

- Towing vehicle
- Unit load carriers
- Pallet trucks
- Fork-lift trucks
- Light-load transporters
- Assembly line vehicle

5.11.1.1. Towing vehicle

A towing vehicle is a vehicle that is used to tow another object, such as a trailer. A motorized ground vehicle, ship, creature, or individuals can be the towing source, and the object being transported can be something that can be dragged. Towing using large pickup trucks is a popular use for these types of vehicles. Towing can be accomplished through a chains, ropes, bar, and hitch, or other mechanism that secures linked objects while in motion. Pulling consists of tractor-trailer configurations, disabled or otherwise inappropriate vehicles, and freight or recreational vehicles hooked to smaller automobiles and trucks with pintle, gudgeon, or the ball hooks. The act of joining two or more objects so they can be dragged by a certain power source is known as a tow service. Anything that can be dragged can be the load being towed, and anything from a motorized land vehicle to a vessel, an animal, or even a person can be the towing source. Different components of towing vehicle are shown in Fig. 5.9.

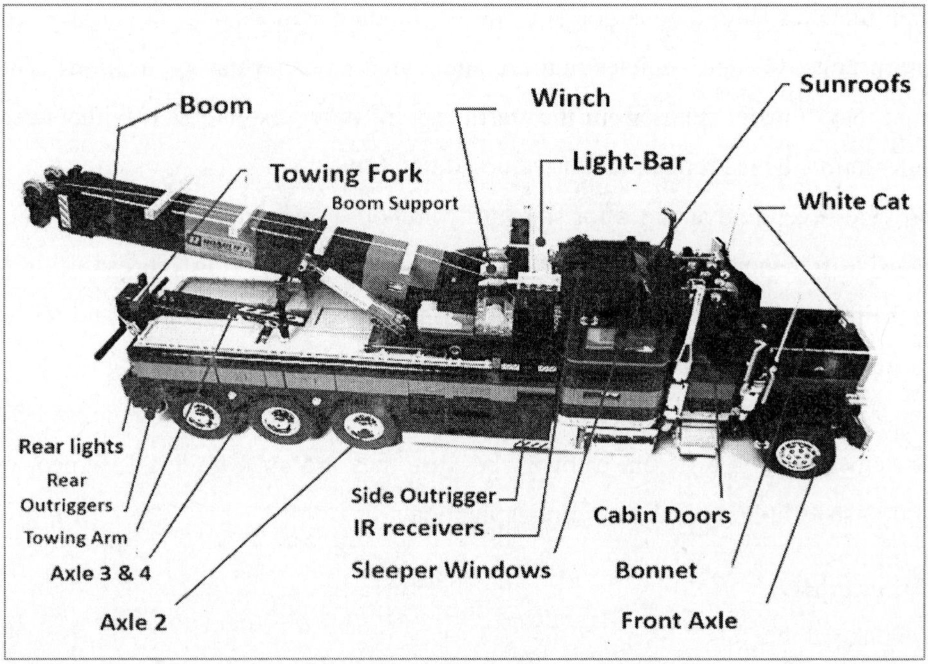

Fig. 5.9. Towing vehicle

5.11.1.2. Unit load carriers

Load carriers and unit loads AGVs are two of the most common kinds of automated guided vehicle systems. They are made to move large, unitized components between manufacturing plants and storage. An autonomous load carrier's design permits loads to be transferred onto the device and then transported over a predefined path. The capacity of automated load carriers and weight carrier automated guided vehicle systems to improve the flow of materials and streamline workflows is one of its main advantages. Companies that automate the load transportation system may eliminate the need for manual labor, lowering the risk of operator mistake and enhancing efficiency. This kind of automated guided vehicle is especially beneficial in companies which demand regular moving of large loads, and especially warehouses and distribution centers.

A cargo pallet or container designed exclusively to carry mail, luggage and freight into an aircraft is called a unit load device. Large volumes of goods can be safely and securely transported by using these technologies to wrap and fasten them onto a single transportable unit. Unit load carrier is shown in Fig. 5.10.

Fig. 5.10. Unit load carrier

5.11.1.3. Pallet trucks

The motorized pallet truck as shown in Fig. 5.11 serves as the primary working equipment in the warehouse, carrying out numerous essential tasks such mobilizing pallets, processing orders, unloading and loading vehicles, and even more. These vehicles support a range of reach trucks, Counterbalanced Forklifts, Trucks, and extremely narrow equipment that have been placed all across the warehouse. This position is crucial since these additional tools tend to be more specialist and sometimes dedicated to a specific assignment or warehousing location.

For high-volume products, machines are capable of shifting two or three pallets simultaneously. They can also frequently work in lines as short as two and a half meters, with or without platforms. Pallet handlers, sometimes referred to as three or two, may be mentioned. While a pedestrian stacking truck functions equivalent to a regular operated pallet truck, it can also lift loads and arrange the items on different levels of rack. Similar to a rider-operated pallet vehicle, a low-level item picking is driven by lifting the person who operates it into the operator's seat with the goal to reach low-level shelving for picking orders. Pallet truck is depicted in Fig. 5.11.

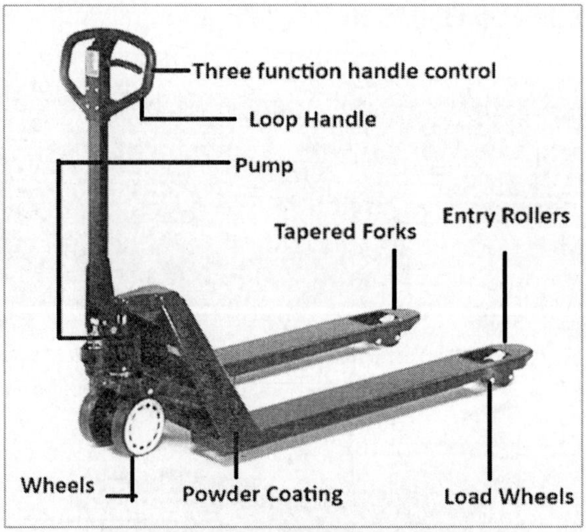

Fig. 5.11. Pallet trucks

5.11.1.4. Fork-lift trucks

It is a mechanized commercial truck made for lifting and moving objects over short distances. It is also known as a fork hoist, lifting truck, or forklift. Forklifts are extensively utilized in manufacturing operations, storage facilities, and mining. Several firms, which developed hoists, and Clark, which made transmissions, came up with the idea for the forklift early in the 20th century. After World War II, forklift trucks gained popularity and underwent development all around the world in the following decades. Forklifts are now considered to be essential equipment in the manufacturing and logistics sectors. Forklifts are small industrial vehicles that can lift and carry cargo due to their motorized front attachment, which can raise and lower the platform.

Many sectors, including warehousing and enormous facilities for storage, employ forklifts to meet their demands. An electric battery or a combustion engine can power a forklift. While operating and managing the machine, some forklift operators can sit, while others have to stand. Across industries, this technique is used to transport a broad variety of commodities and goods. Forklifts can only lift certain loads because of their maximum weight and forward centre of gravity limits. This information is on the nameplate, as indicated by the manufacturer, and the load cannot be greater than these limitations. Consult the manufacturer before changing or removing the forklift's nameplate, as this is prohibited in many places. Rear-wheel steering is crucial to a forklift's operation.

Undoubtedly, this enhances mobility in narrow corners, but this experience is not what an individual is used to from other automobiles with wheels. The instability of forklifts is another crucial aspect. The load and the forklift's center of gravity must be viewed as a single entity with a continuously shifting center of gravity with each load movement. A forklift should never be permitted to turn quickly when carrying a high load, as the cargo will be at its sides. Gravitational pull as well as centrifugal force could topple the forklift. It is important to remember that load undercutting and fork elevation cause the forklift's load limit to fall. Fork lift is demonstrated in Fig. 5.12.

Fig. 5.12. Fork-lift trucks

5.11.1.5. Light-load transporters

They are employed to distribute small, light objects between storage and several work locations by moving them across moderate distances. Systems for light loads can be fully integrated with other systems for manufacturing or logistics. The designed device's capacity to adjust to certain conditions and requirements makes it highly functional. The industrial plant's handling system significantly lowers the likelihood of unforeseen micro-downtimes. They are used to transport small, light items amongst storage and multiple job sites and move them over relatively short distances. Systems for handling light loads easily interface with other systems utilized in production or transportation. The device is highly functional because of its ability to adjust to certain circumstances and needs.

The primary function of the handling system at an industrial facility is to reduce the possibility of unforeseen micro-outages for every processing machine. The light load handling device reduces costs throughout the entire production and delivery process. The process of sorting packaging, order-picking, inspection areas, and storage spaces are all equipped with faultless systems. Light-load transporter is displayed in Fig 5.13.

Fig. 5.13. Light-load transporters

5.11.1.6. Assembly line vehicles

Light-load carriers are accustomed to AGVs assembly line vehicles for applications requiring serial assembly. Important sub-assemblies like motors, transmissions, and sometimes entire cars are transported by the guided vehicle. Further assembly processes are finished when the vehicle moves from one station to the next. The vehicle stops in an assembly area to allow for additional assembly once parts are loaded onto it. The vehicle is released by the operator once the assembly process is finished, and it proceeds to the staging area for the subsequent part.

The vehicle then moves on to the next assembly station. The technique is repeated until the final unloading point has been achieved. The AGVS assembly line has two main advantages over "hard" assembly lines: it is less expensive and simpler to set up. The guidance path can be changed and reprogrammed to easily adjust the line. Programming various dwell times and speeds into the gadget is easy. Nevertheless, comprehensive integration necessitates extensive planning and intricate computer administration. Some of the guiding factors that affect how the AGVs function are as follows:

(i) Guidance Systems ii) AGVS Control Systems iii) Routing iv) Load Transfers v) integrating with additional subsystems. The guidance systems used to keep the car on a predefined course are covered in the section that follows.

Guidance Systems for AGVS: The primary function of a guidance system is to maintain the vehicle on the intended course. The fundamental advantage of an AGVS guidance system is that the guide path may be altered quickly and inexpensively, as opposed to the high expense of replacing fixed-path equipment such as conveyors, chains, and tow lines. Many guidance systems are available, and their selection will be determined by need, application, and environmental limits. Common guidance systems include wire-guided, optical, inertial, infrared, laser, and teaching systems.

AGVs Control System: There are three types of AGVs control systems: (i) computer-controlled, (ii) remote dispatch, and (iii) manual.

Computer Controlled System: The system controller monitors and controls all exchanges, including the movement of AGV vehicles. The AGV's guiding route controller gives input to the process controller. The AGV process controller directly controls the vehicle's motions.

Remote dispatch: AGVS is operated by a human operator through a remote-control console. The vehicle receives destination instructions straight from the control system.

Routing of the AGVs: AGVS routing involves identifying the shortest path between two sites. The typically utilized approaches include: The two ways that are frequently used are the "path switch decision strategy" and the "frequency identification strategy."

Manual Control System: In order to use a manual control system, the driver must start the vehicle and input the destination's address into the onboard control panel. The efficiency of the device is dependent on the operator's skill level.

5.12. Automated inspection and measurement

It is recommended to use an array of 3D measured coordinates from an object provided by a number of sensors being examined, as well as its computer-aided design model, as part of an automated inspection process for manufactured parts. Range sensors are ideal for dimensional verification due to their high precision, fast digitization, and ability to acquire 3D measurements without touching the part. The method begins with registering a set of three-dimensional points with a computer-aided design (CAD) model of the part. Following that, it uses the CAD model to split the 3D coordinates into several surfaces before determining the degree of tolerance to govern the parts.

The inspection results are provided in two ways: as a physical record that details the assessment findings of the tolerances requirements, and visually, as a colour mapping that shows the degree of variation within the measured locations and the model generated by CAD. Two range sensor technologies were evaluated, and the outcomes of the inspection were then compared with measurements made using a coordinate measuring device. The term "automated inspection" describes the process of automating one or more inspection procedures. Automated or semi-automated inspections can be implemented through a number of techniques.

1. An automated handling system displays components automatically. A Manual evaluation and taking decisions come afterwards.
2. Feed parts into the device manually; automatic assessment and making decisions followed.
3. A fully automated inspection system which offers checks and selects components on its own.

5.12.1. Coordinate Measuring Machine (CMM)

In coordinate metrology, the dimensions and shape of an object are measured and compared to those shown on a part drawing. Coordinate metrology assesses an object's position, orientation, size, and shape. An electromechanical apparatus called a coordinate measurement machine is employed in coordinate metrology. It features a three-dimensionally adjustable contact probe that may be positioned in relation to a work part's surfaces. The probe's x, y, and z coordinates can be precisely measured to collect dimensional information on the geometry. The basic CMM includes the following components for measuring in three dimensions:

Probe tip and probes to contact job part surfaces. A mechanical framework that moves the probe in three Cartesian axis and uses displacement detectors to determine the exact coordinates of each axis.

Furthermore, many CMMs contains: The transmission system along with the control unit operate each of the three axis and a digital system for computing that includes application software. Coordinate measuring machine is illustrated in Fig. 5.14.

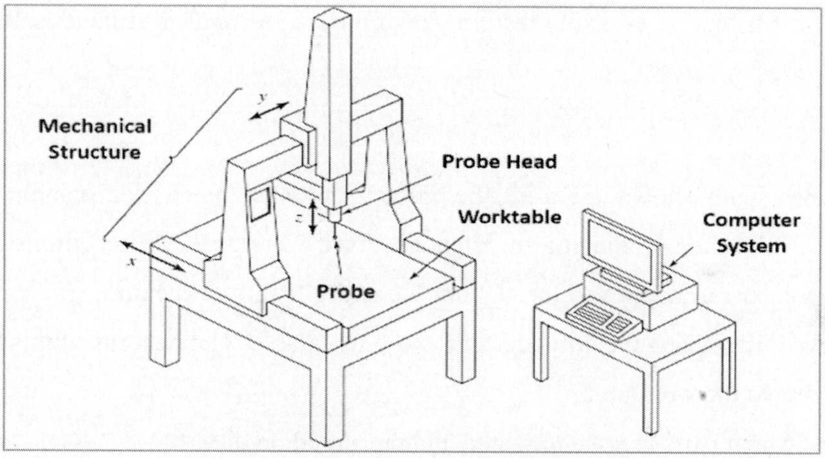

Fig. 5.14. Coordinate measuring machine

5.12.1.1. Construction of coordinate measuring machines

A Coordinate Measurement Systems Probe can move with respect to the component due to its mechanical system. The part is typically assembled on a worktable that is secured to the structure. The two main components of the CMM are the instrument's probe and its mechanical framework.

Probe

During measurement, the contact point of the probe reveals contact with the part surface. Typically, the end of the probe tip is made up of ruby. In this application, strong durability for resistant to wear and low density for limited inertia make ruby an attractive corundum's variety. As can be observed in the illustration, probes can have one or several tips. Nowadays, touch-trigger probes, that engage whenever the probe makes a contact with the part surface, constitute the majority of probes. Touch-trigger probes that are sold widely employ one of numerous prompting methods, such as these: When the probe tip moves out of its equilibrium state, an exceptionally sensitive electrical switch recognizes it. When the probe makes contact with an object, displacement detectors on each of the 3 linear axis correctly measure the probe's location and record it in the CMM controller. The probe tip radius is compensated for, while momentum-induced probe tip overtravel is not considered. After separating from the contact surface, the probe returned to its neutral orientation.

Mechanical configuration

There are several physical configurations for moving the probe, each with strengths and limitations. CMMs that are typically feature one of the six mechanical structures, illustrated in figure.

Cantilever

In the cantilever setup, shown in Figure, the probe is mounted to a vertical spindle that travels in the z-axis, while the horizontal arm extends a fixed worktable. To accomplish the y-axis motion, the pointer can be moved throughout the entire length of the arm, and axis-x motion can be achieved by moving the arm adjacent to the worktable. The benefits of this design are

(1) quick access to the worktable,

(2) the rate of which parts may be mounted and measured on the CMM,

(3) the ability to measure substantial amounts workpieces on massive CMMs, and

(4) relatively lower floor space requirements.

The downside is that it has lower stiffness than many other CMM designs.The measurements' accuracy is lowered by this occurrence. Integrating identical drives and positional feedback mechanisms for both limbs of a movable bridge.

Fixed bridge

The work surface can be moved in the x-direction next to the bridge, which is connected to the Coordination Measuring Machine bed in this arrangement. This construction increases precision and stiffness by preventing the possibility of yawing. However, the extra energy needed to move the heavy worktable with the component fixed on it severely reduces output.

Horizontal arm

A cantilevered horizontal arm connected to a column that is vertical comprises of the horizontal arm arrangement. The arm moves in and out and also vertically to accomplish y- and z-axis movements. Either the work surface or the column must be moved across one another horizontally to generate x-axis movement. In Fig. 5.15, the moving ram notion is demonstrated. Due to its cantilever construction, the horizontal arm structure has a lower rigidity and, consequently accuracy. Positively, it makes getting to the work area better. Large horizontal arm machines are the most efficient way to perform physical measures on automobiles. On some coordinate measuring machines, several arms offer at the same time, separate measures on both sides.

Gantry

Large objects are typically inspected using the structure shown in the figure. The probing nib moves with respect to the horizontal arm that crosses the gantry's two tracks.

Column

The configuration shown in Figure is comparable to that of a machine tool. The worktable moves in the x and y axis, while the probing quill moves vertically along the rigid section in the z axis.

Fig. 5.15. shows construction of six different types of coordinate measuring machines.

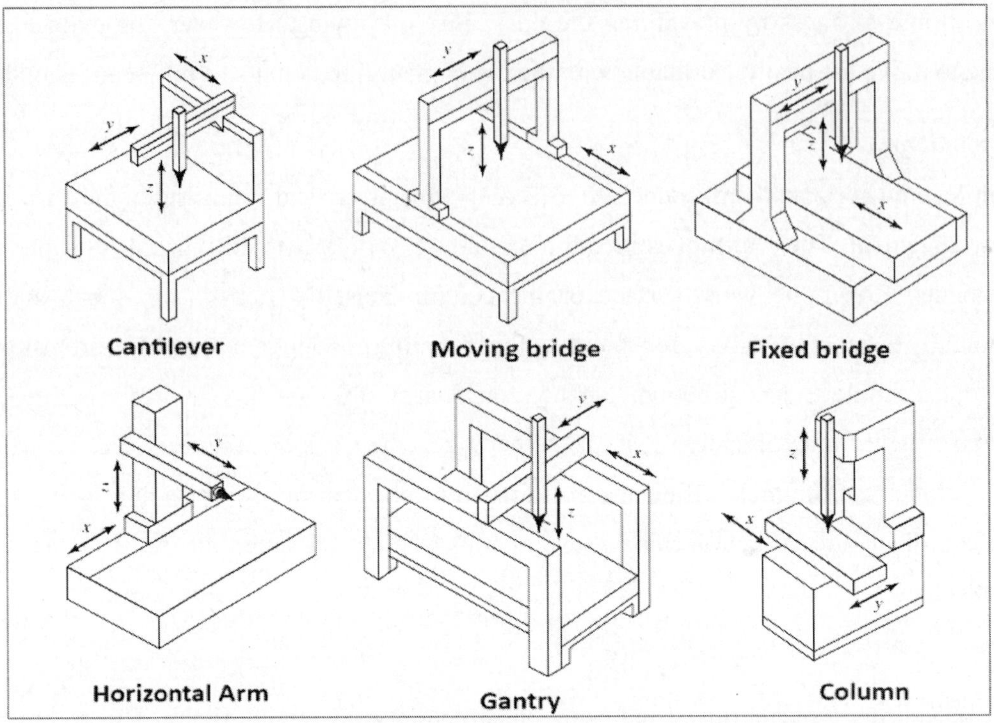

Fig. 5.15. Construction of six different types of coordinate measuring machines

5.12.2. 3D Scanning

3D scanning is the process of gathering information about the geometry and appearance of a physical object, framework, environment, or individual and then converting that data into digital 3D representations. 3D scanners are used to assess objects and environments, collect information, and build models. Several sectors including architecture, engineering, medicine, and cultural activities, use 3D scanning. The process of reverse engineering, computer-assisted design, and additive manufacturing can all be done with 3D scanning. This is only an elementary overview of 3D scanning; there is much more to know about this important tool. Despite the fact that 3D scanning technology vary, each of them follow the same principles. A 3D scanner requires a sensor, which can be a physical probe, a laser, or light, to determine the distance between an image sensor and an object.

Triangulation-based 3D point recognition from images and depth readings is possible with 3D scanners; every single point is shown independently on the screen. The process of projecting an object's shape from its points of view is known as reconstruction efforts. After the database of points is created by the scanner, it is used to create a three-dimensional model made up of surfaces. In simple terms, meshing is the process of connecting a point cloud's vertices to create an accurate view. A mesh is made up of vertices, faces, and details on the connections within the vertices that result in the faces. During the meshing process, one may reduce the priority of some points in order to create a less complicated and consequently better to handle mesh instead of giving each point the same values. The mesh is textured at the end. Texture mapping, sometimes referred to as UV mapping, is the process of applying a texture to a surface. In the context of 3D scanning, a texture is an image printed on a product or service. Every pixel with U and V coordinates in a textured graphic has a matching colour, and the picture files are saved in separate files. A texture-capture camera that gathers colour data everywhere is a common feature of 3D scanners. Optimal outcomes require bright, even lighting, unless the scanner is equipped with a flash. Generally, multiple scans are required to generate a comprehensive model due to the scanner must collect data from all sides of the subject. Scans are combined into a single reference system through a procedure known as aligning or registrations. The images from the scans are then combined to generate a 3D model. The overall 3D scanning process is referred to as the 3D scanning workflow.

5.12.1. 3D Scanning Techniques

- Direct-contact 3D Scanning
- Laser Triangulation 3D Scanning
- Organized Light 3D Scanning
- 3D Scanning Using Laser Pulses
- Photogrammetry

5.12.1.1. Direct-contact 3D Scanning

This technique uses a device called a scanner to directly contact an object and acquire data. When the scanning device investigates an object, it will be either positioned on a surface plate or fixed in place by a fixture. The software that comes with the probes recognizes the manner in which and what point the probe contacts the object's surface and accumulates its three-dimensional position. The coordinate measuring equipment performs as a 3D scanner that depends upon contact. Contact-based 3D scanning is frequently used in manufacturing, particularly for inspections to verify product quality during maintenance or after manufacture.

Although this technology is quite exact and may be used to scan three-dimensional reflective or clear surfaces. It is not appropriate for scanning unstructured objects and is slower than most alternative techniques.

5.12.1.2. Laser Triangulation 3D Scanning

This specific kind of 3D scanning employs a single laser pointer or a laser line to scan an object. The 3D scanner projects a laser, which changes course after reflecting off the object. Through the use of trigonometric triangulation, which the system is able to determine the specific angle of deviation by recording the change in trajectory through a sensor. The scanner may create a 3D scan by mapping the subject's surface after a sufficient number of laser scans. An accurate 3D scanning method that produces high-resolution data is laser triangulation. The primary limitation is that objects with shiny or clear surfaces cannot be scanned with it. Environmental investigations are often conducted using the use of laser triangulation scanners.

5.12.1.3. Organized Light 3D Scanning

Organized light scanners employ the same trigonometric triangulation technique as laser triangulation scanners to produce scans. Instead of using a laser, this method covers an item with a series of linear light patterns. Two sensing cameras assess the length of each line formed by analyzing the light patterns to calculate the distance to the subjects. Subsequently, the scanner can calculate precise X-Y-Z coordinates to generate highly precise 3D models. Organized light 3D scanning is quick, takes excellent pictures, and may be used to scan people. The negative aspect is that it performs inadequately outside since it is highly sensitive to illumination.

5.12.1.4. 3D Scanning Using Laser Pulses

This technology, known as time-of-flight scanning, uses light speed and sensors to construct a scan rather than triangulation. Laser pulse-based 3D scanners measure the time it takes for a cast laser to reach an object and reflect back to the source. As the laser and sensor gear rotates by a mirror, the programme can collect 360 degrees of data and store the information required to generate a three-dimensional model. The fundamental advantage of laser pulse-based scanning is the ability to scan exceedingly vast objects, environments, and systems. However, it is slower than other 3D scanning techniques.

5.12.1.5. Photogrammetry

A technique called photogrammetry uses high-resolution images to extract measurements and other dimensional pertaining to locations and products. Movable or aerial cameras that take a sequence of overlaying pictures of an object can be used for photogrammetry. By analyzing the geometric intersections of light beams and applying triangulation in order to understand data like angles of view, locations, and object properties, photogrammetry applications may subsequently create 3D models. Although this method is used in many other industries, it is particularly helpful in engineering, forestry, mapping, and farming. Although it has numerous benefits, such as high accuracy, cheap cost, and the ability to reach challenging locations, it is also subject to weather and environmental constraints.

5.12.2. Applications of 3D Scanning

3D scanning is used by various organizations and will become increasingly important as software and scanning capabilities progress across industries. These are the primary applications for three-dimensional scanning:

- The entertainment industry
- Health Care
- Architectural design
- Building and Engineering
- Historical Research and Archiving
- Designing
- Forensic Science

5.12.2.1. The entertainment industry

To create 3D models for movies, large displays, and gaming firms, 3D scanning is employed. It is widely used in virtual cinematography in movies and TV shows, where it can swiftly scan objects in the real world. Sculpting real-life model's prior 3D scanning them is a common practice among artists as opposed to individually producing digital versions using 3D modelling tools. 3D scanning has a similar application in the gaming industry, where technology is used to create characters that are used objects, and environments, as well as games that uses virtual reality. It can build realistic 3D models of individuals, objects, and spaces, making it suitable for creating immersive and engaging virtual gaming environments.

5.12.2.2. Health Care

The use of 3D scanning is growing in the health care industry. The ability to create and customize braces, splints, surgical implants, and other wearable technology is one of its biggest benefits. For instance, prosthetics may now be made more accurately, increasing patient comfort, and more affordably than with conventional methods, all thanks to 3D printing. Among other things, 3D scanning is mostly utilized in dentistry to design dental implants. One noteworthy use of 3D scanning in medicine is the creation of 3D images for obstetrics using 3D ultrasound.

5.12.2.3. Architectural design

Using 3D scanning technology allows architects to examine and analyze entire buildings in enormous amounts of detail. Point cloud data from 3D scanners, which are similar to those used in construction, can be utilized to make extremely accurate measurements and visualizations. 3D scanning and CAD software are far faster and less expensive than earlier techniques. Architects may reverse engineer a building's whole structure from the outside to the inside by using 3D scanning.

5.12.2.4. Building and Engineering

In engineering and construction, 3D scanning is extensively used. One of the primary industries to embrace 3D scanning was aerospace, and today it's a common tool in almost all manufacturing, engineering, and construction processes. For instance, it helps with quantity surveys, historical site documentation, and site modelling in the building industry. In engineering, it helps with equipment inspection and reverse engineering. One particularly interesting use of 3D scanning is reverse engineering.

The majority of parts manufactured several decades ago are only described in two-dimensional drawings, which makes accurate reproduction challenging and time-consuming. Nevertheless, 3D scanning makes it possible to gather extremely precise data about an object's geometry, which can subsequently be used to build a new 3D model. This model can then be used to generate new castings and tooling, allowing manufacturers to make entirely novel components with exactly the same dimensions as the original. These reverse-engineered designs can also be utilized to create 3D printed replicas of the original. For example, 3D scanning can be used to restore historic automotive parts that are no longer accessible. Although 3D scanning eliminates much of the guessing and is significantly quicker than conventional reverse engineering, the procedure is exceedingly efficient, and the findings are highly accurate.

5.12.2.5. Historical Research and Archiving

Historical researchers, scholars of art, and archaeologist are widely using 3D scanning to document and analyze their findings. 3D scanning generates reversible, extremely accurate 3D representations of artefacts and works of art, making it a significant technology for archiving and curating. Furthermore, it enables the dissemination of exact copies throughout the research and educational communities. 3D modelling is also valuable for historical study; for example, it is frequently used to reconstruct the face traits of humans' evolutionary forebears using fossil scanning techniques.

5.12.2.6. Designing

For many product designers, reverse engineering and rapid prototyping are essential steps in the design process, which makes 3D scanning an invaluable resource. 3D scanning is a fast and accurate method that allows designers to explore intricate combinations and produce new designs while simulating natural materials. Moreover, 3D scanning makes it possible for scans to be shared online, generates incredibly precise results with complex forms and elements, and makes it easier to coordinate the manufacture of products using components from many sources.

5.12.2.7. Forensic Science

The use of 3D scanning by authorities as a forensic technology is expanding. It is known for its ability to produce incredibly accurate models of shooting scenarios, incidents, bloodstain sequences, and bullet trajectory. In this context, 3D scanning can be utilized for analysis as well as documentation.

5.13. Machine vision

Machine vision is a method of replicating the human system's visual identification and analysis skills using electronic and electromechanical approaches. A machine vision system allows for the identification and alignment of a workpiece within the field of vision, and it has multiple applications. It can be used in a variety of robotic systems, not just for automated inspection.

Machine vision involves acquiring picture data of an item of interest, analyzing it, and interpreting it using a computer program for practical applications. The term "machine vision" describes any industry or non-industrial activity in which a hardware and software integration gives machines instructions on how to operate while they carry out tasks based on the gathering and examination of images. Similar methods and strategies are used in industrial machine vision, although with various limitations, for administrative, military, and scholarly applications. When compared to academic or educational vision systems, industrial vision systems are typically more dependable, long-lasting, and cost-effective.

They are also frequently less expensive than vision systems used in government or military operations. Thus, low prices, moderate precision, robust resilience, high reliability, and remarkable mechanical and thermal durability are associated with industrial machine vision. In machine vision, cameras are used to gather visual data from their environment. After that, it uses a combination of hardware and software to process the images, readying the data for use in a range of applications. In machine vision technology, specialist optics are often used to acquire images. This method makes it possible to process, analyze, and keep a focus on specific visual attributes. For instance, a production system's machine vision application can be used to look at a certain attribute of an object as it is being made on an assembly line. It may determine whether the part satisfies requirements for product quality and, if not, dispose of it.

5.13.1. Machine Vision Stages

Inspection primarily involves gauging dimensions, measuring, and verifying component presence. The operation of a machine vision system, as shown in Figure, involves the following four vital stages:

- Image creation and digitization.
- Image Processing and Analysis.
- Image interpretation.
- Generation of actuation signals.

Fig. 5.16 indicated machine vision stages.

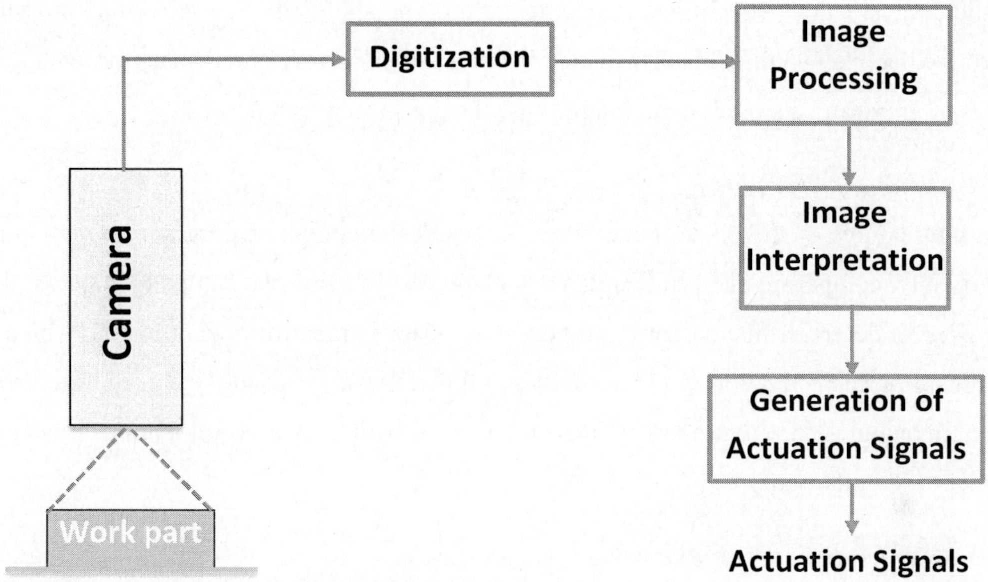

Fig. 5.16. Machine Vision Stages

5.13.1.1. Image creation and digitization

The main job of a vision system is to take a 2D or 3D picture of the workpiece. For simple inspection tasks, a 2D picture shows a work part from above or from the side. A 2D image can be taken with a single camera, but a 3D image needs two cameras, one in each place. The work-portion is positioned on a level surface and is well-lit so that there is a noticeable contrast between the piece and its surroundings. A sharp image is captured after the camera is trained on the work area. The image is made up of a matrix of distinct picture pieces, sometimes known as pixels. Every pixel in the scene has a value that corresponds to the amount of light present in that area. An analog-to-digital converter converts each pixel's intensity value to its corresponding digital value.

5.13.1.2. Image Processing and Analysis

Every single pixel's status is stored in the frame buffer. There are numerous approaches available for visual data analysis. For more research, the data in the frame buffer must be processed and refined.

The most widely used method of image processing is segmentation. Edge detection and thresholding are the two phases of segmentation. Thresholding uses the light intensity to determine if a pixel value is black or white. We call this vision system a binary system. Several shades of grey can be stored in an image using the grey-scale technique.

5.13.1.3. Image interpretation

Once the features of the object have been extracted, the computer programme may quickly identify it by comparing them to templates that are kept in memory. Template matching is the term used to describe this matching process. An object is identified via a match, which also permits further investigation. The interpretation function used to identify objects is referred to as pattern recognition. Creating templates or databases with known object features is necessary in order to identify patterns.

5.13.1.4. Generation of actuation signals

The vision system should tell the inspection station what to do when it detects an object. When working in a flexible inspection environment, work pieces are moved from machining stations to inspection stations and vice versa by the work-cell controller sending actuation signals to the transfer machine. Actuation signals for clamping, declamping, gripping, and other operations on work components are produced by the work-cell controller.

5.14. AI and machine learning

Artificial intelligence (AI) and machine learning (ML) are two closely related fields that are revolutionizing human-technology interaction. The technique of teaching computers to learn from data without having to be particularly programmed to do so is known as machine learning. This involves employing statistical models and algorithms to find patterns in data, which are then used to inform judgements or predictions. Conversely, machine learning and other methods of creating intelligent systems fall within the broader category of artificial intelligence. The goal of artificial intelligence is to create machines that can carry out tasks that would typically need human intelligence, like speech recognition, understanding natural language, and making sophisticated data-driven decisions.

Machine learning and artificial intelligence aim to create computers capable of acquiring knowledge and adapting to new environments without the need for specific programming. By allowing computers to learn from data and make decisions based on it, one can create algorithms that tend to be more accurate, productive, and efficient performing a range of tasks. The creation of systems that can learn from and respond to new environments without the need for specific programming is the aim of both machine learning and artificial intelligence. self-driving vehicles, artificially intelligent assistants, healthcare diagnosis, and identifying fraud are all examples of applications that use machine learning and AI.

As technology progresses, we may see more innovative applications of machine learning and artificial intelligence in the future. Machine learning and artificial intelligence are causing a lot of enthusiasm around the globe. The enormous range of uses for artificial intelligence has changed the face of technology. The terms machine learning and artificial intelligence are often used interchangeably. Artificial intelligence and machine learning are two distinct but closely linked fields. The development of statistical models and techniques that enable computers to learn and make decisions without explicit programming is known as machine learning, a branch of artificial intelligence (AI).

Using data, machine learning algorithms can be trained to find patterns and forecast future occurrences. However, the phrase artificial intelligence is broader and encompasses machine learning as well as other methods of creating intelligent systems. The development of computer systems with artificial intelligence (AI) allows them to do tasks like understanding natural language, identifying objects, and making decisions tasks that would typically need human intelligence.

5.14.1. Basic difference between artificial intelligence and machine learning:

However, there is a substantial difference between the two that industry experts do not fully understand. Artificial Intelligence refers to when a computer system performs intellectual tasks. Machine Learning, on the contrary, is a type of AI that learns from data, including information acquired from prior experiences, and allows the computer programme to adjust its behavior accordingly. Artificial Intelligence is a combination of Machine Learning, that means although every machine learning is AI, not every AI is machine learning. There are several categories into which machine learning is divided, including:

Supervised learning: Training the algorithm on a labelled dataset that already has the desired output is known as supervised learning.

Unsupervised learning: The system has to figure out the underlying structure on its own without being given tagged data.

Reinforcement learning: The algorithm gains knowledge by interacting with a particular environment and analyzing the feedback it receives.

Artificial Intelligence (AI)	**Machine Learning (ML)**
Artificial Intelligence handles larger-scale concerns related to system automation. Such computing might be achievable using any field, including image processing, brain research, neural networks, machine learning, and so on.	Machine Learning influences users' computers to learn from their surroundings. Such surroundings can include sensors, electronic components, storage devices that are external, and a variety of other devices.
AI facilitates the development of intelligent machines, frameworks, and other devices by allowing them to think and do tasks in the same way that humans do.	ML analyses to see if the customer's query or input from the user is already in the knowledge base. If it is accessible, it will return to the user the answer to that query; but, if it isn't originally saved, the system will receive the user's input and build its knowledge base, providing the user with a more valuable experience.
The goal is to maximize the chances of success.	The goal is to increase accuracy.
Decision trees and logic are used in artificial intelligence.	Statistical models are used in machine learning.
Understanding machine behavior and the dissemination of knowledge are vital elements of AI.	Knowledge acquisition is a focus of machine learning.
Aims to build robots with mental and cognitive abilities similar to those of individuals.	Allows algorithms and systems to gather information from their data exposures to enhance over time.

Artificial Intelligence (AI)	Machine Learning (ML)
AI combines several concepts related to intelligence, such as preparation, estimation, and perception.	Machine learning can be performed using reassurance, without supervision, or controlled techniques.

5.15. Human machine interfaces (HMI)

A human-machine interface (HMI) is a user interface that allows a machine or process to interact with a human operator. Human Machine Interface (HMI) is commonly used in industrial areas including factories and power plants to monitor and control activities. A human-machine interface can take many different forms, such as computer user interfaces with graphics, touchscreen devices, and real-time control panels with controls and displays.

In addition to displaying additional information and alerts, they are utilized to show the operator process data so they can enter commands and setpoints. A programmable logic controller is often coupled to a human-machine interface to control the process by gathering data from field sensors and the human-machine interface. On the human-machine interface, the operator can observe information and issue commands. The programmable logic controller receives these commands and executes them.

5.15.1. Human-Machine Interface Types

Human-Machine Interfaces (HMI) are classified into many different categories and can take various shapes based on the application's requirements. Some popular forms of human Machine interfaces are:

5.15.1.1. Graphical User Interfaces (GUIs): GUIs are computer-based human-machine interfaces that show process data and respond to operator commands. GUIs can be created using software such as Microsoft Windows or a dedicated Human-Machine Interface program.

5.15.1.2. Touchscreens: These human-machine interfaces utilize a touchscreen display to show process data and allow the user to enter commands. They are commonly used in situations where a physical control panel is impractical, such as in confined places.

5.15.1.3. Physical Control Panels: These are actual HMIs that demonstrate process data and allow users give instructions through displays, keys, and controls. They are frequently used in industrial settings where a user interface or touchscreen would be difficult due to strong vibration or dust.

5.15.1.4. Web-based Human-Machine Interfaces: These are human-machine interfaces that display process data and allow operators to enter commands through a web browser. They allow users to remotely observe and regulate processes using any device that can access the web.

5.15.2. Benefits of Human-Machine Interfaces

Human machine interfaces are useful for monitoring and regulating industrial processes due to a number of benefits it offers.

5.15.2.1. Increased Efficiency: By making it simple for users to access process data and enter commands, human-machine interfaces help to increase the efficiency of the process that is under control. When data is presented in an easy-to-understand manner, operators can respond faster and make better decisions.

5.15.2.2. Enhanced Safety: By providing the operator with alarms and other important information, Human-Machine Interfaces can increase safety. This makes it possible for operators to proactively address any problems before they get out of hand.

5.15.2.3. Remote Observation and Control: Although many human-machine interfaces are remotely accessible, an operator can keep a close watch on and oversee processes from a distance. This is especially important if the procedure is located in a remote or hazardous area.

5.15.2.4. Easy to use: Human-machine interfaces are made to be as simple to use as possible, especially for operators who are not very tech-savvy. As a result, they are an effective instrument for overseeing and controlling industrial operations.

5.15.3. Limitations of Human-Machine Interfaces

The following possible disadvantages should be taken into account when choosing whether to use a human-machine interface:

5.15.3.1. Dependency on the Human Machine Interface: The process being controlled may not go as intended if the user is unable to see the information being processed or to offer commands due to a malfunction or outage of the human machine interfaces.

5.15.3.2. Possibilities for Human Error: Human error can take the form of mistyped commands or ignored notifications when utilizing a human-machine interface. This could lead to issues with the regulated procedure.

5.15.3.3. Additional Cost: The acquisition and deployment of the Human Machine Interface as well as any necessary equipment and software might be expensive when implementing one.

5.15.3.4. Complexity: Some Human Machine Interfaces are complicated, which makes them challenging to operate or demands for further user learning. This could be a disadvantage in applications where the person in charge needs to be able to process commands and process data quickly and easily.

5.15.4. Applications of Human-Machine Interfaces

Human machine interfaces are utilized in a wide range of industrial applications to help increase the productivity, security, and accessibility of the process under management. Some common applications of Human-Machine Interfaces are:

5.15.4.1. Manufacturing: Manufacturing operations, including those on the plant floor, are often controlled and monitored using human machine interface in manufacturing contexts. They are frequently utilized to display alarms and other pertinent information, allow users to enter instructions and parameters, and present process data.

5.15.4.2. Power Generation: Whether a power plant uses renewable or fossil fuels, human machine interface is used to monitor and manage processes like electricity generation and distribution, boiler operation, and turbine control.

5.15.4.3. Water and Wastewater Treatment: The pumping process, treatment, and delivery are just a few of the operations that human machine interface controls and monitors in these facilities.

5.15.4.4. Oil and Gas: Human machine interfaces are used for tracking and controlling operations including the drilling process, pumping, and processing in the production and processing of oil and gas.

5.15.4.5. Chemical Processing: Processes like mixing, reaction, and distillation are monitored and controlled by human machine interface in chemical processing facilities.

Unit Summary

This unit discusses digital, inclusive, smart, and distributed manufacturing, including Industry 4.0, digital transformations on shop floors, CIM to smart factory, intelligent machines to smart machines, factory automation to distributed automation, and human sense to system sensed.

Solved Examples

1. Write a short note on AGVs guiding system.

Ans1. The goal of an AGVs guidance system is to maintain the AGV's predefined path. Compared to conveyors, chains, and other systems, one of the main advantages of AGVs is the ease with which the guidance system may be altered to alter the guiding path at a low cost. The variable nature of the guiding path, which permits path overlap, is another benefit. The leading path typically doesn't interfere with other systems. The selection of guidance systems can be contingent upon the AGV type, application, specifications, and environmental limitations.

2. Define briefly modern AGV features.

Ans2. Modern AGV features are listed below:

1. Contemporary AGVs are microprocessor-equipped, computer-controlled vehicles.
2. Set up the feedback mechanism to the right course.
4. Utilising system controllers to communicate between automobiles
5. Computers for system management
6. Making the best use of AGVs
7. Monitoring the material undergoing transfer and controlling AGV movement.

3. Where do AGVs find application?

Ans3. Various commodities can be moved by these AGVs at various phases of production:

Lines of Assembly: Raw materials can be transported from material shelves to assembly line workstations using towing AGVs. For instance, these vehicles are capable of transporting huge trucks loaded with steel, aluminium, motors, batteries, brakes, fuel tanks, and other automotive components.

Packaging Lines: Semi-finished items like televisions and washing machines can be lifted and moved from assembly to packaging lines using Forklift AGVs. These goods are being processed and will be packaged for delivery.

Logic Warehouses: Unit Load AGVs can move finished goods from packaging lines to logic warehouses or dispatch stations, including groceries and beverages packed in boxes.

4. What are some common applications for automated guided vehicles?

Pallet Handling: AGVs are widely used for pallet handling. These responsibilities include loading, unloading, stacking, and moving pallets, resulting in an efficient material handling procedure across the plant.

Work-In-Progress Movement: In work-in-progress movements, AGVs deliver unfinished materials between stages of production. AGVs in work-in-progress movements, for example, often convey supplies from one location in a facility to an assembly line during the manufacturing process. Companies that embrace industrial automation can use AGVs to improve workflow efficiency and minimise the need for manual handling during the assembly process.

Trailer loading: AGVs are frequently used to speed up the process of loading products from assembly lines or storage facilities into trailers that are ready for export. Specialised equipment, such as lifting platforms or conveyor belts, can be installed on these vehicles to load pallets or containers into trailers quickly and effectively. Consequently, AGVs decrease manual labour and boost overall efficiency while improving loading speed and accuracy.

Exercises

Q1. Differentiate between hydraulic and pneumatic systems?

Q2. What do you mean by sensors integration?

Q3. Explain pick and place robots with a neat sketch.

Q4. Explain welding robots with a neat sketch. Write down its advantages.

Q5. What do you mean by human machine interface. Also write down its advantages, limitations and applications.

Q6. Differentiate between artificial intelligence and machine learning.

Q7. Define briefly gears and its types.

Q8. Explain different types of belt drives in detail.

Multiple Choice Questions

1. How do "IoT" and internet technologies fit into the framework of Industry 4.0?
   a. They offer the framework for tying common commodities together
   b. They lay the groundwork for production that is environmentally sustainable
   c. They act as an essential component of business interaction

2. What is the commencement date of Industry 4.0?

   a. 2007 b. 2010

   c. 2013 d. 2016

3. When was the term "Industry 4.0" originally introduced?

   a. 2009 b. 2010

   c. 2011 d. 2012

4. When was the Third Industrial Revolution initiated?

   a. 1950s b. 1960s

   c. 1970s d. None of the above

5. In which year did Prime Minister Narendra Modi introduce the Make in India initiative to improve India's manufacturing industry?

   a. 2013 b. 2014

   c. 2015 d. 2016

6. A Mechanisation is a _______.

   a. When a machine is operated by a human

   b. When machines carry out duties in place of humans

   c. Putting machines into people

   d. Improving machine technology

7. The assembly line was invented by whom?

   a. Andrew Carnegie

   b. Cornelius Vanderbilt

   c. John D. Rockefeller

   d. Henry Ford

8. This company was the first to use a robot's technology on its production line.

   a. Ford Motor Co b. Volkswagen

   c. General Motors d. Toyota

9. What technology led to the First Industrial Revolution?

   a. Steam Power

   b. Electricity and Mass Production

   c. Computers and Semiconductors

   d. Agrarian Riots and Starvation

10. The internet of things, access to real-time data, and the advent of cyber-physical systems are the major advances in this period.

    a. The Third Industrial Revolution

    b. Industry 4.0

    c. Manufacturing Age

    d. Industrial Revolution

11. What is the full form of the IOT technology?

    a. Internet of Things b. Idea of Things

    c. Integration of Things d. Institute of Things

12. The acronym IIoT stands for __________.

    a. Industrial Internet of Things

    b. Internet Internet of Things

    c. Intelligence Internet of Things

    d. Internal Internet of Things

13. When will the market be opened to industry 4.0?

    a. It is already being used

    b. It will not be used, it just a project

    c. It will be released on 2030

    d. Never, because it is a bad idea

14. Which robotic generation of the guaranteed ones can be controlled remotely?

    a. First b. Second

    c. Third d. None of the preceding

15. Which of the following engineering disciplines deals with the mechanism and structure of robotics?

    a. Electrical b. Mechanical

    c. Computer d. All of the above

16. Which simple level robots come to mind?

    a. Machine for washing

    b. Completely automatic washing machine

    c. Notebook

    d. None of the aforementioned

17. What are the different various types of dynamic robots?

a. One
b. Two
c. Three
d. Four

18. The robots' joints are divided into _________ types

a. One
b. Two
c. Three
d. None of the above

19. How many types of sensors are utilized in industrial robots?

a. One
b. Two
c. Three
d. Four

20. What are the advantages of robotics?

a. No requirement for experience
b. Expensive
c. Requires a large power supply
d. Replaces human workers

21. Which of the following joints has translational motion?

a. Orthogonal Joint
b. Rotational Joint
c. Twisting Joint
d. None of the above

22. Which of the following requires the least number of integrations?

a. Robot
b. Cobot
c. Both a and b
d. None of the above

23. Which one of the following sections in robot manipulator used for orientation of objects?

a. Body & arm
b. Wrist assembly
c. Both a and b
d. None of the above

24. Which of the following robots is considered second generation?

a. Information robots
b. Autonomous loading
c. Water Inspection
d. None of the above

25. Which one of the following joints comes under rotary motion?
    a. Orthogonal Joint
    b. Linear Joint
    c. Both a and b
    d. Revolving Joint

Answers for multiple choice questions:

Keys for multiple choice questions: 1(a), 2(c), 3(c), 4(b), 5(b), 6(b), 7(d), 8(a), 9(a), 10(b), 11(a), 12(a), 13(a), 14(a), 15(b), 16(b), 17(c), 18(d), 19(c), 20(a), 21(a), 22(d), 23(b), 24(b), 25(d)

KNOW MORE

For more information related to this topic scan the QR code,

OR

Type this link in your browser

https://ufile.io/byrek4n5

References

1. https://archive.nptel.ac.in/content/storage2/courses/downloads_new/ 112104289/noc20 _me 44_assigment_12.pdf

2. https://archive.nptel.ac.in/courses/112/106/112106179/

3. https://onlinecourses.nptel.ac.in/noc23_ee87/preview

4. Mikell P. Groover, Automation, Production Systems and Computer Integrated Manufacturing, Fourth Edition, Pearson. USA (2015).

6 ADVANCED AUTOMATION TRENDS

UNIT SPECIFICS

Industry 4.0 brings about a transformation in the industrial sector, where modern automation trends are used as a tool to complete tasks. This chapter provides a detailed summary of the advanced automation trends.

RATIONALE

Knowledge of advanced automation trends and its implementation is required in fully automated industries, one must know about these trends and techniques.

PRE-REQUISITE

Knowledge of automation tools and techniques

UNIT OUTCOMES

List of outcomes of this unit is as follows:

U6-O1: Students should be able to understand digital, inclusive, smart and distributed manufacturing

U6-O2: Students should be able to know about Industry 4.0

U6-O3: Students should be able to understand digital transformations in shop-floors, CIM to smart factory, intelligent machines to smart machines, factory automation to distributed automation, human sense to system sensed.

Unit Outcomes	Expected Mapping with Programme Outcomes *(1- Weak Correlation; 2- Medium correlation; 3- Strong Correlation)*					
	PO-1	PO-2	PO-3	PO-4	PO-5	PO-6
U6-O1	3	1	3	1	1	2
U6-O2	3	3	2	2	2	3
U6-O3	3	3	1	2	1	3

A thorough explanation of Industry 4.0, digital shop floor transformations, and robots is covered, along with an introduction to digital, inclusive, smart, and distributed manufacturing. Intelligent machines to smart machines, industrial automation to distributed automation, and CIM to smart factory. This chapter defines human senses in relation to system senses.

6. Advanced Automation Trends

These trends demonstrate the ongoing changes in production brought about by advances in technology and the need for adaptability and agility. These are a few significant developments influencing the technological evolution of the manufacturing sector such as digitalization and industry 4.0, artificial intelligence, additive manufacturing, sustainable manufacturing, robotic process automation, autonomous mobile robots, collaborative robotics, dark factories, deep learning-powered vision, enterprise resource planning technology and industrial internet of things.

6.1. Digital Manufacturing

The use of digital technologies into the production process is known as digital manufacturing. The effectiveness, quality, and flexibility of production are enhanced through the use of data, automated processes, and linkages. A comprehensive approach to manufacturing, digital manufacturing leverages computer technology to enhance production processes. Manufacturing facilities are using an increasing number of automated tools; therefore, in order to optimize processes, industries require computerized back-office systems that can track, assess, and simulate each unit of equipment.

Digital manufacturing aims to achieve effectiveness, flexibility, efficient design, and collaboration. Computer-based tools and systems are being utilized to enhance manufacturing processes as digital technologies gain importance in a variety of global firms. Among other things, bottlenecks, storage facilities, and production times might be reduced with real-time data. The manufacturing industry is undergoing a digital transformation that is commonly referred to as Industry 4.0 or the fourth revolution. This shift enables firms to optimize production processes and boost global competitiveness.

6.1.1. Important facets of digital manufacturing include:

- Smart Factories are production processes that are optimized through the use of sensors, IoT devices, and real-time data analytics.
- The technique known as additive manufacturing, or 3D printing, uses digital plans to create objects layer by layer while minimizing waste and enabling customization.
- Before real production begins, industrial processes are tested and optimized using digital simulations.
- Using robots to do tasks including material handling, assembly, and quality assurance.
- Cyber-physical technologies refer to the combination of computer technology and physical machines that provide smooth control and communication.

6.1.2. Benefits of digital manufacturing:

The manufacturing sector can profit from digital manufacturing in a number of ways, as the following are listed:

6.1.2.1.Enhanced efficiency: Errors resulting from inaccurate data, which are common in manual or paper-based operations, are avoided in an integrated, digitalized manufacturing process.

6.1.2.2. Rapid innovation: Innovations happens more quickly because to advanced technology, which includes modernized equipment and IT systems that may be connected to provide analysis of data and visibility.

6.1.2.3. Satisfied customers: Digital manufacturing increases brand awareness and loyalty by enabling businesses to remain in tune with their customers' needs and wishes.

6.1.2.4. Reduced expenses: Inventory levels and delivery statuses can be adjusted to cut costs at every stage of the production process with more control and understanding of the supply chain.

6.2. Inclusive Manufacturing

A new paradigm known as "inclusive manufacturing" aims to accelerate sustainable growth and encourage dignified wellness for everyone by making products available to people from all social classes at every step of their lifecycle. The purpose of inclusive manufacturing is to make it possible for people, particularly those who are economically, physically, socially, historically, or traditionally underprivileged, to actively participate in the production, distribution, use, and disposal of goods and systems.

Promoting an equitable and transparent environment in the manufacturing sector is the aim of inclusive manufacturing. The new paradigm of inclusive manufacturing involves producing useful goods and pertinent services that are within everyone's means. Its goal is to derive value from the endeavours by utilizing all available types of technology. Encourage honorable well-being in all the various social production facets. This is so that the most common unmet requirements are always envisioned to be fulfilled, and the qualities of diligence, inquiry, and proximity are effectively combined in Inclusive Manufacturing.

Consequently, Inclusive Manufacturing takes into account particular investment goals, fosters suitable partnerships, develops feasible paths, and peacefully self-mitigates the likelihood of various problems related to this shift. Pre-manufacturing efforts that are proactive in being inclusive promote accountability, and post-manufacturing endeavours that are sustained foster sustenance.

Inclusive manufacturing has several advantages that encourage economic development and progress in society are discuss below.

6.2.1. Advantages of Inclusive Manufacturing:

Let us look at some of the advantages:

6.2.1.1. Job Creation and Economic Growth: Millions of well-paying jobs might be generated if the manufacturing industry is restored. Creating work reduces inequality and empowers underprivileged groups. Manufacturing accounts for 20% of overall capital expenditure, 30-40% of productivity growth, 60% of exports, and 70% of corporate R&D costs. Growing this industry can significantly boost economic growth.

6.2.1.2. Resolving Supply Chain Issues: Manufacturing has the ability to alleviate widespread supply chain concerns, especially during current unpredictable global times. Strong manufacturing leads to enhanced global competitiveness over time.

6.2.1.3. Innovation and Digitization: An industrial revival can be sparked by embracing innovation and digitization. Contemporary technologies increase output, reduce expenses, and create new opportunities for fair growth. In industrial firms, fostering a diverse and inclusive culture fosters creativity and adaptation, leading to better business outcomes.

6.2.1.4. Positive Effect on Societies: By generating stable employment and fostering economic stability, inclusive manufacturing helps underprivileged communities. It ensures more equitable distribution of wealth and strengthens regional economies.

Apart from the financial gains, an inclusive approach creates a positive work environment, fosters empathy, and raises corporate morale.

6.2.2. Key components of inclusive manufacturing consist of:

Following are the key components of inclusive manufacturing:

- Increasing the breadth of skills, genders, and ethnicities represented in the workforce is known as diversity and representation.
- Equipping people with the information and training required to operate in the manufacturing sector is known as skills development.
- Establishing workspaces that are accessible to people with disabilities is referred to as creating accessible workplaces.
- Guaranteeing that workers are fairly compensated, enjoy safe working conditions, and follow moral guidelines.

6.3. Smart Manufacturing

The goal of smart manufacturing is to optimize the entire industrial environment through the use of data, automated processes, and networking. The term "smart manufacturing" describes the collaborative, efficient, information-driven, and event-driven coordination of company operations, physical, and digital operations in factories, plants, and along the value chain. Using sensing, information, process modelling, predictive analytics, and workflow, smart manufacturing integrates, monitors, and continuously assesses resources and processes to automate routine tasks and recommend actions for non-routine circumstances. Organizations, people, and technology come together in smart manufacturing to create solutions that are secure, scalable, responsive, open, semi-autonomous, coordinated, resilient, and long-lasting.

The operational efficiency of the manufacturing ecosystem is significantly improved by smart manufacturing, leading to quantifiable increases in output, rapidity, flexibility, safety, quality, asset reliability, and energy productivity. Enhanced profitability encourages more spending on innovation.

6.3.1. Elements of Smart Manufacturing:

IIoT sensors: A sensor receives information in real time, including how many parts are moving past a conveyor belt in front of it. In combination with predetermined parameters such as the belt's life expectancy, it can generate a more accurate maintenance plan. Thus, it can be changed without interfering with processes during downtime, avoiding the requirement for substitution of functional parts due to a static maintenance strategy or the expensive delays brought on by an operational failure.

Cobots: An autonomous robot fleet receives a signal; the human operator need not control the fleet or be aware of which bot completes the task. After identifying the nearest and most appropriate unit, the algorithm automatically adopts safety behaviors, such stopping when a human teammate crosses its path.

Digital twins: To assist with the placement of elements based on their proximity to power distribution channels, entry points like doors, and other factors, it can make a digitalized three-dimensional model of the entire process and connect it to local geographical information system evidence when adding an additional product line to a plant.

6.3.2. Benefits of Smart Manufacturing

- Improved measurement and control of operations through sensors and big data.
- Increased employee satisfaction as their own work becomes more valuable and less repetitive.
- Improved productivity, which saves money and can be invested in product development.
- More manufacturing jobs.
- Improved sustainability.
- Operational equipment efficiency.

6.3.3. Important features of smart manufacturing include

- IoT integration, which involves linking devices, equipment, and sensors to gather data in real time.

- The application of data analytics to forecast equipment failures and reduce downtime is known as predictive maintenance.
- Supply chain visibility refers to tracking materials, parts, and finished products all the way through the supply chain.
- Real-time decision-making involves using data to get quick, well-informed conclusions.

6.4. Distributed Manufacturing

Unlike centralized factories, distributed manufacturing produces goods in widely dispersed geographic locations. Distributed manufacturing involves corporations leveraging technology to connect geographically separated production units. Distributed manufacturing allows value generation in spatially dispersed places in organizational structures. Merchandise that has been created in very close proximity to their intended marketplaces, for instance, might reduce shipping costs. Small businesses dispersed throughout a vast region can also customize goods to suit local or personal preferences. Coordinating the supply chain to put together parts made in several real locations is also regarded as a form of distributed manufacturing. Decentralized and spatially distinct production is made possible by digital networks and additive manufacturing, which is often referred to as "cloud manufacturing."

6.4.1. Benefits of Distributed Manufacturing

6.4.1.1. Faster turnaround times: the duration between making and selling goods can be reduced with decentralized manufacturing. Companies may deliver parts to the customers more quickly by minimizing supply chains and delays in shipping by producing products closer to the point of demand.

6.4.1.2. Reduced production costs: The most economical way to manufacture goods in traditional manufacturing is to produce large quantities of them. Even when producing in smaller quantities, costs can be cut by lowering waste, transportation, and customs fees.

6.4.1.3. Enhanced sustainability: Products will not need to travel as far to reach customers when production is moved to decentralized plants, which might reduce the company's carbon impact. Lower-volume production can also assist minimize waste since it produces the least amount of excess material waste during manufacturing and can prevent part degradation brought due to significant quantities of orders. This is especially true when employing 3D printing technology.

6.4.1.4. Increased adaptability: Digital manufacturing improves supply chain efficiency. Various plants that comply with high-quality requirements permit rapid pivoting in reaction to unanticipated occurrences such as shortages of supplies or trade route interruptions affecting product availability.

6.4.2. Important aspects of distributed manufacturing include

- Local manufacturing reduces transportation costs and environmental impact by producing goods close to the point of consumption.
- Facilitating small-scale production on demand to meet specific client needs.
- The ability to quickly reorganize supply chains in reaction to interruptions or shifting demand is referred to as agility.
- Manufacturing, suppliers, and customers are connected globally through digital platforms.

6.5. Industry 4.0

Industry 4.0, also referred to as smart manufacturing, is the term used to describe how the manufacturing industry has evolved technologically. Decision-making in real time, enhanced output, adaptability, and mobility are made possible by it, revolutionizing the way companies produce, enhance, and market their goods. Industry 4.0 is an emerging revolution in which web-based communication technologies are integrated with many parts of industrial networks to create the smart workplaces and manufacturing organizations of the coming years. Innovation that disrupts is currently driving Industry 4.0 and its associated technology, which has the potential to create plenty of fresh possibilities for the creation of value across every significant market area.

The adopters of Industry 4.0 will face considerable obstacles and hurdles due to the cybersecurity and data privacy concerns affecting modern Internet technology. Industry 4.0 will face cybersecurity and privacy challenges that are both old and new. Industry 4.0 may never reach its full potential if these problems are not resolved. The fourth industrial revolution has begun for the world economy today. The main economies are eagerly embracing the transition to Industry 4.0, even though it is nonetheless in its early phases and cutting-edge digital technologies are still being created and deployed. This is due to emerging technologies and the possibilities that present are generating a great deal of interest. Germany was the first country to create a national strategic strategy aimed at Industry 4.0 in 2012. The UK came next, having accepted Industry 4.0 as the industry's primary area of growth and envisioned "outstanding innovations".

6.5.1. Elements of Industry 4.0

In general, Industry 4.0 refers to the expanding trend of automation and data interchange in manufacturing technologies and processes, which includes: IoT, smart sensors, advanced robotics, big data analytics, 3D printing, augmented reality, cloud computing, location tracking, machine learning, predictive maintenance and quantum computing as shown in figure below.

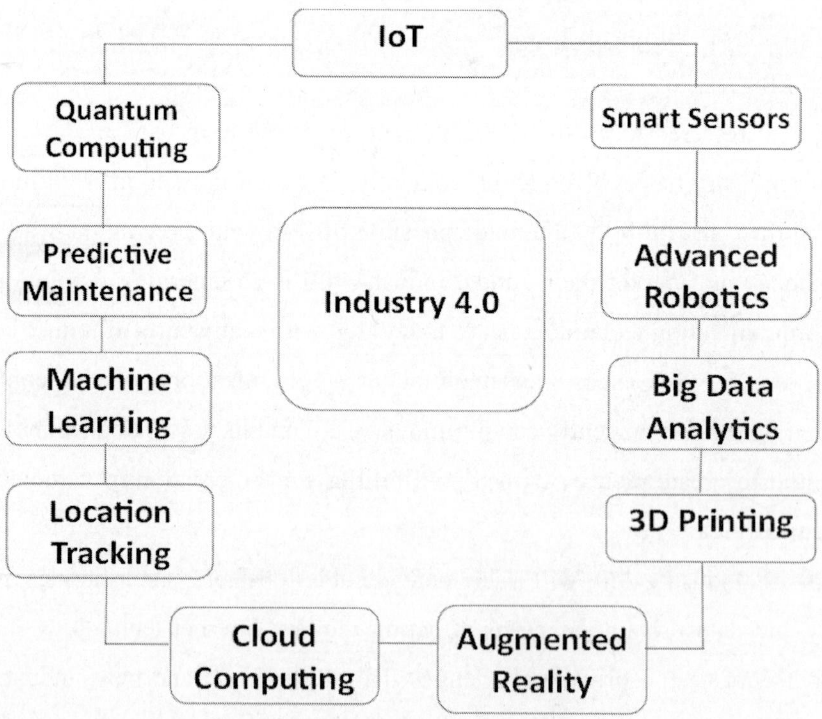

Fig. 6.1. Elements of Industry 4.0

6.5.2. Benefits of Industry 4.0

- Increased output and reduced machine breakdown
- Enhanced productivity
- Enhanced security and supply chain management
- Better product, line, and factory lifecycles with digital twin utilisation
- People with empowerment
- Enhanced cooperation and exchange of knowledge
- Flexible and agile

6.5.3. Disadvantages of Industry 4.0

- High prices
- Elevated failure rate
- Online safety measures
- Demand for highly qualified workers
- Market and Businesses Disruption

6.6. Digital transformations in shop-floors

The most important development in recent years has been the technology revolution. It offers a multitude of options and novel approaches to tasks. One sector of the economy that digital technologies have completely transformed is manufacturing. The integration of digital technology into production processes is known as "shop floor digital transformation" in manufacturing, and it is a component of the ongoing technological revolution. In the manufacturing industry, digital shop floor transformations are becoming more and more significant. Shop floor digital transformation is necessary for small and medium-sized businesses in order to stay competitive.

The top major companies in cutting-edge technology have already made an impact. The conversation about the shop floor's digital transformation doesn't end here. Data on smart technology's ability to generate revenue, however, refutes this notion. The shop floor's digital transformation gives businesses a competitive edge. It's up to small and medium-sized firms to decide how much money to put in and how quickly to increase their efforts at digital transformation. Putting up with change will only result in absoluteness. Customized smart technology is offered by several service providers.

6.6.1. Fundamentals of digital transformations on the shop floor

The practical foundations of digital transformation for the shop floor are as follows.

6.6.1.1. Communication Centralization

A small part of the motivation behind the digital transformation of the shop floor is cognitive. People have to change the way they think about conventional methods. Increase data sharing

and dismantle data barriers. Investment in a digital framework that allows an industrial plant to have centralised communication. For instance, the greatest choices for sharing and consolidating data are offered by cloud servers. Invest in affordable hosting services so that each performer can use a single mouthpiece to communicate. Use data-sharing technologies to enable communication between human actors and machines.

6.6.1.2. Smart Technology

Achieving digital shop floor transformation is challenging due to the multiple tangible human interactions in the supply chain. One can reduce our dependency on human labor by substituting technological innovations for these kinds of services. This reduces errors made by humans and boosts productivity. Moreover, consistent output is made possible by process automation. Resource management is improved by artificial intelligence and digital sensors. Wait times and unheard-of malfunctions are decreased by smart technologies. By increasing equipment uptime, orders may be delivered on time.

6.6.1.3. Utilising and Storing Data

The creation of enormous amounts of data is necessary for the digital transformation of shop floors. Due to this, companies need to have the infrastructure in place to use data and give management access to it. The foundation of the store for transformation is data management and storage. Cloud servers, for instance, provide massive storage capacity. They make it accessible from anywhere at any time. The ability to access remote data allows managers to monitor shop floors from any location. Remote sites can send instructions to keep production lines running.

6.6.1.4. The interconnection

Interconnectivity is emphasised in the shop floor's digital revolution. It covers elements of manufacturing-related business management. The goal of shop floor transformation is to enhance the relationship between operations management, machine performance, and order placement. Thus, the basis of the shift is building a platform to oversee this interconnection. Business and machine data are integrated in the analytics dashboard. These are significant analytical centres where managers may monitor workflow and equipment performance.

6.6.1.5. Enhancement of Functional Effectiveness

The main goals of the digital transformation of the shop floor are linkages. It aims to boost the effectiveness of operations. The aim of any firm is to maximize revenue while cutting expenses. Because of this, the foundation of any shop floor makeover is efficiency optimization. Thus, efficiency is increased by the use of Industry 4.0 infrastructure. Digital sensors, automation, IoT, and artificial intelligence are a few of these. These technologies maximize manufacturing efficiency and reduce material waste.

6.7. CIM to Smart factory

The transition to smart factories depends heavily on computer-integrated manufacturing. CIM systems are essential to the production of electronics. To carry out production activities, optimise the supply chain, and ensure product quality, they bring together a variety of computer systems, automated robotics, and technical specialists. The goal of Industry 4.0 and the Smart Factory is to seamlessly integrate business and production processes so that operations can be optimised on their own and continuously.

Manufacturers of Surface Mount Technology equipment have expanded the capabilities of their CIM systems beyond managing single machines. These days, they handle whole production lines as well as related tasks like material handling. Establishing a general smart manufacturing method is beneficial in order to lower complexity and cost.

We may divide the current CIM applications into three fundamental layers: 1. Specific manufacturing processes are managed through the use of process applications. 2. Factory operations are managed through site applications. 3. Industrial operations are linked to broader corporate processes through enterprise software. To realise the concept of a Smart Factory, manufacturing facilities must invest in:

IIoT sensors: These collect information from legacy machines.

CIM Devices: These allow institutions to easily implement innovative technology for digital transformation.

A particular manufacturing process is managed or controlled by Process Applications, the lowest layer. These include applications from machine vendors, sensors, PLCs (programmable logic controllers), or custom apps that manage operations, gather data, or give instructions to someone or a process. Process applications can demand data from higher-level infrastructure, such work orders, flow control, or material information, or they can provide event data that is helpful to other processes.

The site Applications oversee the whole manufacturing flow, including work order details and material information needed for process-specific operations, and they are positioned above process-specific applications. Manufacturing execution system architecture, process engineering, quality control, material management, and limited production planning tools are examples of site-level functions. These applications are typically used to actively manage production operations by consuming event data produced by certain processes.

6.7.1. Benefits of CIM to Smart Factory

The major benefits of CIM are listed below:

Increased Reliability and Efficiency: Manufacturers can gather data on equipment and processes in real time by using sensor networks and CIM devices. If there are any deviations, notifications are generated immediately. Based on the collected data, manufacturers can quickly change the specifications of the equipment.

Streamlined Production Processes: By combining different manufacturing tasks, CIM streamlines production. An automated and more synchronised manufacturing system results from better coordination.

Decreased Expenses: CIM assists in lowering labour costs, both direct and indirect. Cost savings are aided by decreased downtime and increased scheduling flexibility.

Sustaining Appropriate Stock Levels: CIM guarantees precise inventory control, averting shortages or overstocking.

6.8. Intelligent Machines to Smart Machines

A smart machine is one that believes, solves challenges, generates decisions, and behaves using cognitive technology and/or machine-to-machine innovations, including artificial intelligence, deep computing, or machine learning. Robots, self-driving automobiles, and other cognitive computing systems are examples of intelligent equipment that can carry out activities without the need for human intervention. These technologies give businesses a competitive edge that should lead to higher profit margins and more efficient manufacturing processes. Intelligent devices have long been in our technological environment.

Machine intelligence was in use long before the phrase artificial intelligence came into existence in the 1950s. Jobs that had previously only been done by human operators were gradually supplanted by early motorized machine tools that were precisely constructed and programmed by skilled professionals. These machines showed signs of basic intelligence by changing and getting more powerful. Still, the term "artificial" sometimes conjures up negative emotions such as inauthenticity or inferiority. Some claim that artificial intelligence isn't really artificial because it was invented by humans, behaves like a human, and has a substantial impact on human lives.

AI can be used to handle a wide range of problems, from complicated mathematical problems with a single correct answer to real-world scenarios with several variables that change over time. Diverse intellectual groupings may come to different conclusions when developing AI for the same goal. Think about scenarios where a violent dictatorship is supported by one AI design and a benign democracy by another. When developing AI, choosing the right "brains" is crucial, especially when working with potentially self-governing military systems. creating automated weapons with audit records to guarantee control and accountability. Make sure autonomous functions act in a way that is predictable to human operators. designing learning and adaptable systems with a clear ability to justify their decisions and reasoning.

6.8.1. Benefits of Intelligent Machines to Smart Machines

Following are the benefits of intelligent machines to smart machines:

Enhanced Efficiency: Higher productivity and more efficient operations are the outcome of smart machines' ability to perform tasks faster and more accurately than people.

Cost reduction: Smart robots can reduce operational expenses and free up human resources for more strategic work by automating repetitive procedures.

Enhanced Accuracy: More precision and dependability are achieved by smart machines since they minimise errors, especially in data-intensive activities.

Improved Decision-Making: These devices are capable of analysing vast volumes of data, spotting patterns, and offering insights to support individuals in making wise choices.

Continuous Operation: Unlike humans, intelligent machines are able to work continually without stopping for breaks or relaxation.

Multitasking: They are adept at managing several tasks at once, which boosts productivity.

Memory and Information Retrieval: Smart devices are able to swiftly recover information from a variety of digital sources because to their superb memory.

Adaptability: They are able to change with the times and gain knowledge from past mistakes.

6.9. Factory Automation to Distributed Automation

Factory automation refers to the use of technology and control systems to automate various processes within a manufacturing facility whereas distributed automation employs an alternative methodology. Rather than centralising control, it disperses control and decision-making among different parts and subsystems. Factory automation encompasses a wide range of applications, including assembly lines, robotics, conveyors, and quality control.

In distributed automation, all machines, gadgets, or subsystems are given the ability to control and make decisions. In order to improve dependability and efficiency in power distribution networks, distributed automation systems make use of automated systems and contemporary technologies. Another name for it is a distributed control system (DCS). A distributed control system is a computerised control system that usually consists of many autonomous controllers dispersed throughout the system and multiple control loops, without the need for supervisory control from a central operator.

A distributed control system is not the same as a centralised control system since its control functions are dispersed across multiple controllers instead of being housed in one place. Distribution automation refers to the method by which utilities apply controls after automatically collecting and analysing data. Distribution automation (DA) is a set of technologies that enables a utility to collect, automate, analyse, and optimise data in order to improve the operational efficiency of its distribution power system.

Several important distribution system operations, including fault detection, feeder switching, and outage management; voltage monitoring and control; reactive power management; preventative maintenance for vital substation and feeder line equipment; and grid integration of distributed energy resources, can be sped up, cost-effectively decreased, and accurately performed with the help of distribution automation. These technologies include switches, processors, sensors, and information and communication networks. Products comprise the systems and parts needed to oversee, gauge, keep an eye on, and control the electrical loads on distribution systems and distribution substations, including:

- Optimisation of assets
- Equipment that is networked and automated
- Distribution Optimisation Demand Optimisation
- Software for monitoring, controlling, and analysing distribution systems
- Networks for information and communication technologies
- To guarantee product certification and compliance, test systems and equipment.

6.9.1. Benefits

Following are the benefits of distributed automation:

Decreased Line Loss: Close coordination between apparatus, distribution feeders, and related devices can help the distribution substation, which acts as the network's electrical centre, reduce line losses. Volt/VAR control can be implemented using expert algorithms, which lower line losses and boost system reliability.

Enhanced Power Quality: Distribution automation helps to keep power quality constant throughout distribution feeders. By identifying and resolving power-related issues before they have an impact on customers, the substation's Remote Terminal Unit and power monitoring tools raise customer satisfaction.

Planned Capital Expenses: Utilities can schedule maintenance more effectively by including preventive maintenance algorithms into the system. This results in delayed capital spending by reducing human costs, optimising equipment usage, and extending equipment life.

Optimal Energy Use: Real-time control, as part of a fully integrated automated power management system, enables calculations to cut demand charges. Load-shedding algorithms also optimise utilities and different power sources while taking into account electricity costs.
Economic Benefits: Distribution automation improves system efficiency, allowing utilities to operate more closely to their systems' physical constraints. This leads to more efficient system utilisation and economic benefits.
Improved dependability: Automation elements like load shedding and automatic control functions help to increase dependability by shortening outage times.
Compatibility: Distribution automation solutions can be incorporated into existing infrastructure, allowing them to work with outdated systems.

6.10. Human Sense to System Sensed

Human senses produce a symphony of perception, but the technology is able to precisely distinguish binary whispers. Eyes see faces, colours, and the sky; sensors, on the other hand, count electrons in certain places. Whereas voltage spikes and circuit spins are examples of system senses, touch is a delicate tango among textures and skin. Without an embrace, silicon nerves throb as fingers searches for warmth and elegance.

The system uses unusual algorithms, recognises sounds in the atmosphere, and analyses data packets. Transistors pulse and interpret everything around them, and ears tuned to music, laughing, and whispering. With binary bits and zeros rushing through the system, taste is a thrill to experience. The tongue combines flavours of sweetness, savouriness, and spices. Circuits, on the other hand, are distantly hungry and only taste voltage. Aroma, sweet recollections, the embrace of nostalgia, and the system's recognition of ones and zeroes in cyberspace. Stories of roses, rain, and pine are inhaled by noses, but code fragments lack a scent design. System senses are precise, unwavering, and have a binary line, but human senses are complex, flawed, and divine. They combine to produce a symphony of virtual and real worlds.

6.10.1. Benefits of human sense to system sensed

In technology and human-computer interaction, this expression refers to the benefits of combining human senses with computer systems or AI. A few instances are presented here.

6.10.2. Assistive technology and access

Individuals with visual impairments can access textual content via text-to-speech technologies like screen readers. Touchscreens' haptic feedback, which gives tangible indications, allows users to connect with devices more effectively.

6.10.3. Health and wellbeing

Wearable fitness trackers and health software monitor heart rate, steps, sleep habits, and other parameters to support healthy living. Telemedicine platforms enable clinicians to consult with patients remotely, increasing access to healthcare.

6.10.4. Safety and Security

By identifying people or spotting intruders, surveillance cameras and facial recognition software improve security. Smoke and fire detectors warn residents when they detect danger.

6.10.5. Customisation and Suggestions

Algorithms for recommendations gain knowledge from user preferences to offer customised recommendations. Social media companies curate personalised content using sentiment analysis.

6.10.6. Efficiency and Automation

By modifying the lighting, temperature, and appliances according to occupancy or the time of day, smart home solutions maximise efficiency and automation. By cutting waste and raising productivity, industrial sensors enhance production processes.

6.10.7. Environmental Monitoring

To encourage environmental preservation, sensors keep an eye on pollutants, water levels, and air quality.

UNIT SUMMARY

This section covers digital, inclusive, smart, and distributed manufacturing, including Industry 4.0, digital transformations on shop floors, CIM to smart factory, intelligent machines to smart machines, factory automation to distributed automation, and human sense to system sensed. Smart automation systems and their various types are described as well.

Solved Examples

1. Write down the advantages of decentralised manufacturing.

Ans1.) It's hardly surprising that companies are implementing decentralised manufacturing methods given all the advantages distributed manufacturing offers. The following are a few of the main benefits of distributed manufacturing.

Faster response times: The time between production and sales can be shortened with decentralized manufacturing. You may deliver parts to your clients more quickly by cutting supply chains and shipping delays by producing products closer to the point of demand.

Reduced production costs: The most economical way to manufacture goods in traditional manufacturing is to produce large quantities of them. Even when producing in smaller quantities, costs can be cut by lowering waste, transportation, and customs fees.

Enhanced sustainability: Your products would travel less to reach your customers if production is moved to decentralised plants, which might reduce the carbon footprint of your business. Lower-volume production can also help minimise waste by producing less surplus material waste during manufacturing and by reducing part obsolescence caused by high order numbers, especially when using techniques like 3D printing.

Increased flexibility: Distributed manufacturing increases the supply chain's agility. When numerous manufacturers are able to provide your parts to the highest requirements, one can turn fast. Furthermore, you will have the ability to act quickly in the event that uncontrollably occurring situations injure your things, such as trade route obstacles or shortages of materials.

2. Discuss the suggestions for managing a successful distributed manufacturing process.

Ans2. Following are the suggestions for managing a successful distributed manufacturing process:

Data Security

This system relies on one single primary component, which must be emphasised: data. Next, after you receive the client's file, is sending the design file to the nearby manufacturer. The mother firm and the local manufacturer exchange data constantly while the product is being manufactured. For your parts manufacturing business to succeed, protecting this information also referred to as intellectual property—is crucial. Businesses are now considering blockchain technology as an intriguing solution, even though there are numerous programmes and tools available to assist with data protection.

Effective Systems of Communication

Data protection is important, but so is communication. During the production process, data transmission back and forth is important. It makes it easier to communicate the crucial ideas needed to complete the job successfully. Workplace communication tools like Salesforce Chatter and Microsoft Teams are great examples.

Encourage the Use of the Same Technology Platforms

Encourage consistent use of technology platforms throughout production sites to avoid issues with inconsistent use. This could complicate communication concerns and the collection of vital data. With the same communication technology used across all facilities, it is much easier to communicate and protect data exchanged across the platform.

Search for Good Companies

If you do not use the correct production business, all of the elements listed above will be irrelevant. This is why you must employ the best companies accessible. Rapid direct provides one of the highest quality parameters available elsewhere in the world. As a result, working with us provides you with all of the benefits of producing overseas.

Exercises

1. Write down the various types of advanced automation trends used in automation industry?
2. What do you mean by digital manufacturing? Write down its benefits and limitations.
3. What is inclusive manufacturing? Write down its key components and advantages.
4. Discuss smart manufacturing in brief. Write down its benefits and salient features.
5. What are important aspects of distributed manufacturing?
6. Describe industry 4.0, its elements, advantages and disadvantages.
7. Write down the fundamentals of digital transformations on the shop floor.
8. Explain distributed manufacturing in detail.

Multiple Choice Questions

1. Which components make up the automation pyramid of a smart factory?

   a. Control b. ERP

   c. Manufacturing Execution System d. All of the above

2. The Manufacturing Execution System (MES) is

   a. A company management software that enables planning, order processing, supply chain management, sales and distribution, and accounting functions

   b. Enables production reporting, scheduling, dispatching, product and labour tracking, performance analysis, quality management, resource allocation, and so on

   c. A computer system that collects and analyses real-time data while monitoring, controlling, and optimising industrial plants

   d. All of the aforementioned

3. Which of the following is Computer Integrated Manufacturing's goal?

   a. Increase number of employees

   b. Integration of different products

   c. Integration of islands of automation

   d. Segregation of manufacturing cells

4. Which of the following has the widest scope within an organisation?

   a. CAM b. CAPP

   c. CAD d. CIM

5. Which is not a component of computer-integrated manufacturing?

   a. Mining b. Marketing

   c. Warehousing d. Product design

6. Which is not one of the ten automation and process improvement strategies?

   a. Manual operations b. Online inspection

   c. Simultaneous operations d. Specialization of operations

7. Which is not a component of computer-integrated manufacturing?

   a. Mining b. Marketing

   c. Warehousing d. Product design

8. Which of the following functions are classified as advanced automation functions?

   a. Material handling b. Welding

   c. Error detection and recovery d. Assembly

9. A Smart sensor is an appliance that utilizes a ____ to assemble specific data along a physical condition to achieve a determined & programmed task?

a. Amplifier

b. Transducer

c. Conductor

d. None of these

10. The Communication function allows the sensor to exchange with the specific ___?

a. Microcontroller

b. Amplifier

c. Op-amp

d. None of these

11. Which of the following is not an essential part of an IoT system?

a. Sensors

b. Communication and data processing

c. User interface

d. Transformer

12. A ____sensor is a type of substance used to monitor, measure, and control liquid levels.

a. Pressure

b. Temperature

c. Optical

d. Level

13. What is a full range of Internet of Things (IoT) devices for homes that includes smart switches?

a. Belkin's WeMo

b. Cinder

c. Awair

d. Canary

14. What types of sensors are used to provide exact measurements of liquid extent?

a. Point level
b. Continuous level

c. Terminated level
d. None of these

15. Smart sensors are frequently preferred over mounted sensors since they have fundamental ___capacity?
    a. Actuating
    b. Processing
    c. Higher
    d. None of these

16. Direct measurements are made in order to identify physical waves and convert them into _____ signals?
    a. Electrical
    b. Magnetic
    c. Mechanical
    d. None of these

17. The point level sensor is employed to define if a liquid has attained a required point inside a ______?
    a. Container
    b. Switch
    c. Temperature
    d. None of these

18. What is the use of a fixture in manufacturing?
    a. Heat treating components
    b. Securing workpieces during machining or assembly
    c. Transporting components between machines
    d. Lubricating machine parts

19. What is the major purpose of ergonomics in manufacturing?
    a. Improve production speed
    b. Create ergonomic workspaces and tools
    c. Automate manufacturing processes
    d. Lower manufacturing costs

20. What is the main purpose of an industrial robot in manufacturing?
    a. Perform repetitive operations with precision
    b. Design products
    c. Conduct quality control checks
    d. Manage inventory

Answers for multiple choice questions:

Keys for multiple choice questions: 1(d), 2(d), 3(c), 4(d), 5(b), 6(a), 7(b), 8(c), 9(b), 10(a), 11(d), 12(d), 13(a), 14(b), 15(b), 16(b), 17(a), 18(b), 19(b), 20(a)

KNOW MORE

For more information related to this topic scan the QR code,

OR

Type this link in your browser

https://ufile.io/g4qo4u5e

References

1. Mikell P. Groover, Automation, Production Systems and Computer Integrated Manufacturing, Fourth Edition, Pearson. USA (2015).
2. https://onlinecourses.nptel.ac.in/noc20_me44/preview
3. https://onlinecourses.nptel.ac.in/noc21_me120/preview
4. https://onlinecourses.nptel.ac.in/noc21_mg83/preview

7 Examples and Case Studies

UNIT SPECIFICS

This chapter offers examples and case studies of advanced automation techniques frequently employed in modern enterprises.

RATIONALE

These examples provide the insight and information related to the topics cover under manufacturing automation.

PRE-REQUISITE

Nil

UNIT OUTCOMES

List of outcomes of this unit is as follows:

U7-O1: Students should be able to understand pick and place robots

U7-O2: Students should be able to know about testing and sorting based systems

U7-O3: Orientation of parts: in-bowl and out-of-bowl toolings

Unit Outcomes	Expected Mapping with Programme Outcomes *(1- Weak Correlation; 2- Medium correlation; 3- Strong Correlation)*					
	PO-1	PO-2	PO-3	PO-4	PO-5	PO-6
U7-O1	3	1	3	1	1	2
U7-O2	3	3	2	2	2	3
U7-O3	3	3	1	2	1	3

Pick and place robots, testing and sorting-based systems, and part orientation: in-bowl and out-of-bowl toolings are all explained in detail. This category covers manufacturing automation with autonomous computer judgements based on data collected from resources and realistic process/machines (production conditions) embedded with digital data driven by adoptive controls.

7.1 Pick and Place Robot

Pick and place robots are some of the most commonly utilized automation equipment in the food packaging sector. Pick and place robots empower organizations to implement automated methods for moving and positioning commodities. Material handling and transportation are straightforward tasks that don't need a lot of preparation. Since the workers can be used for other tasks requiring more mental ability, using people for these professions may not be efficient. These repetitious tasks are handled by pick-and-place robots. Typically, these robots are equipped with sensors and cameras to retrieve objects off moving conveyor belts.

A major turning point in the development of pick and place robots has been reached with Unimate. In 1961, it was the first industrial robot to be programmed. The Unimate was developed by George Devol and Joseph Engelberger. It was capable of carrying out a range of tasks by adhering to a movement pattern that was preprogrammed. It was a six-DOF robot designed to mimic the human wrist, elbow, and shoulder. It led to the development of progressively more sophisticated programmable robots that can carry out difficult tasks with remarkable flexibility and precision.

Delta robots are now the foundation for pick and place robots that perform repetitive operations in the food packing industry. A research team at EPFL in Switzerland, directed by Professor Reymond Clavel, developed the delta robots in the early 1980s. The first packaging pick and place robots were mass-produced in 1987 after Demaurex, a Swiss business, got the manufacturing license. When ABB Flexible Automation introduced the FlexPicker delta robot in 1999, the industry saw a rapid shift. Researchers are currently working to optimize pick and place robots for repetitive activities that require higher precision and speed, as well as for small components that computer processors can pick.

Robots for picking and placing come in a range of designs, based on the use for which they are intended. Most of these designs follow comparable concepts. These robots usually have a long arm that can cover the whole field of action and are installed on a stable platform. The end-of-arm attachment is designed specifically for the kind of object the robot intends to move. These robots can move objects from one stationary surface to another, from one moving surface to another, from one stationary surface to another, and from one moving surface to another. Pick and place robot is shown in figure below.

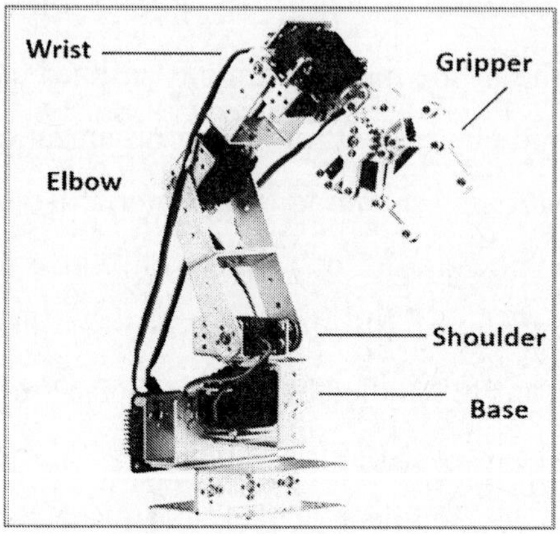

Fig. 7.1 Pick and Place Robot

7.1.1. Components of Pick and Place Robots

Several specialized components make up a pick and place robot, including:

Robotic Arm: A manipulator, sometimes referred to as a robotic arm, is a robot's extension made of spherical or cylindrical elements. joints and connections.

End Effector: The device at the end of a robotic arm that performs a necessary function, such grasping objects, is called an end effector. Depending on the needs, the end effectors can be made to carry out various tasks.

Actuators: The motion of the robotic arm and its end effectors is produced by actuators. Any kind of motor, including stepper motors, servo motors, and hydraulic cylinders, can be used as a linear actuator.

Sensor devices: Sensors can be compared to the robots' eyes. The sensors perform functions such as determining an object's position.

Controllers: Controllers are the brains behind a robot's seamless operation since they coordinate and regulate the movement of the many actuators in the robot.

7.1.2. Types of pick and Place Robots

- Cartesian Robots
- Rapid Pick Robots

- Automated Arms / Robotic Arms
- Delta robots
- Collaborative Robots

7.1.3. Advantages of a Pick and Place Robot

- ❖ One of the main benefits of pick and place robots is their speed of operation. In the time it would take a human worker to raise one object, these machines can lift many objects simultaneously.
- ❖ Robots that pick and place objects are more productive than humans because they can work at a faster pace. Because of this, contemporary manufacturing settings are able to boost production rates and launch more products.
- ❖ The need for pauses for human labour might cause disruptions in the production process. There are also disruptions when employees switch shifts. On the other hand, robots can work day and night and don't need breaks.
- ❖ Human mistake is a constant component of labour performed by humans. On the other hand, a pick and place robot operate based on precise mathematical principles, eliminating errors and producing a consistent output.
- ❖ When lifting something, there is a chance that it will fall on workers and injure them. Robots, on the other hand, do not pose this risk, increasing workplace safety.
- ❖ Pick and place robots require a minimal upfront investment, but they allow businesses to reduce operating costs. Paying salaries or benefits is not necessary. As a result, the production processes yield a higher return on investment.
- ❖ Pick and place robots move a lot of objects in a short amount of time; hence their throughput is higher. Fast pick robots have the capacity to move 300 items each hour, as was previously reported.

7.1.4. Uses for Pick and Place Robots

Industrial robots for food packaging aside, pick and place robots have various uses. Among these applications are:

Assembly Operations: Pick and place robots are used in assembly operations to collect parts from many locations and assemble them in one area. These kinds of pick and place robots are used in complex technological environments.

Packaging: The pick and place robot picks up the food products and places them in a packaging container as a packaging utility. Even better, the objects can be selected from a conveyor belt and loaded into a packaging container.

Bin Picking: Pick and place robots can be used in applications that involve the retrieval of a specific item from a bin. With the help of their sophisticated vision systems, these pick and place robots can precisely identify the necessary item—a function that is necessary for bin picking.

For Proper Inspection and Quality Control: Pick and place robots for inspection and quality control recognise each item and determine if it complies with the manufacturer's quality control guidelines. The robot has the ability to take an item off the production line if it fails.

Sorting of Parts: Depending on an object's shape or the information it contains, robots capable of part sorting can arrange various items. These have comparable uses, such as parcel segregation.

Medicine Sector: Pick and place robots are also finding their applications in the medical sector. They not only help in sorting the medical inventory but can even assist in complex surgeries.

7.2. Testing and Sorting Based Systems

Programmes and specialised tools are used in software testing techniques like automation testing to automate the execution of test scenarios. Creating programmes that mimic user interactions with the software and running them independently are steps in the process that validate its efficacy, dependability, and performance. By automating laborious and manual testing procedures, automation testing offers benefits including faster test execution, more thorough test coverage, and early fault identification. It reduces human error and gives testers more time to work on more complex testing elements. It also facilitates Regression Testing by retesting previously verified capabilities to ensure they remain unaffected by modifications. All things considered, improving software quality, output, and the development strategy requires testing that is automated.

7.2.1. Automation Testing Types

Two primary categories of automation testing types are used in the process of developing software to evaluate various parts of a software application: functional testing and non-functional testing.

Verifying the software's functional characteristics and requirements is the main goal of functional testing. It includes ensuring that the test operates as expected by comparing the software's behavior to the necessary features. The main goal of this kind of testing is to confirm that the programme satisfies user needs and functions properly.

Non-functional testing, on the other hand, evaluates aspects of the software other than its functionality. Performance, accessibility, safety, reliability, and compliance are all assessed throughout this testing.

7.2.1.1. Functional testing

Functional testing involves feeding inputs into the system to determine if the outputs resemble what was supposed to happen or expected. Two of the approaches include black box testing, which focuses mostly on the inputs as well as the results without examining the inside implementation of the process, and white box testing, which involves examining the actual internal framework and coding. Many techniques, such as equivalence splitting, threshold value analysis, decision charts, and user scenario-based testing, are used in the design and execution of functional test cases. The purpose of functional testing is to verify that the software runs properly and accomplishes the required tasks as specified.

Primary objectives of functional testing

The system's stated requirements are validated with the use of functional testing. It makes sure every component of functionality - including processing of data, interaction between users, and systems behavior - aligns with the functionality that is desired.

- Functional testing looks for possible shortcomings, errors, or irregularities in the program by carefully investigating its functionality. This aids in keeping the software operating as intended.
- Functional testing ensures that the programme works as intended in a range of scenarios, including different inputs and user interactions. It ensures that the programme operates

within normal limits, produces correct results, and responds appropriately to human interaction.

- When assessing the software's functionality and user experience, functional testing is essential. To guarantee a seamless and fulfilling user experience, functional components of the programme relating to human interactions, design of interfaces, and system receptivity should be validated.
- The risks connected with software faults or problems are reduced with the support of functional testing. Proactive functional issue detection in the course of the development cycle reduces the likelihood of significant errors or adverse impacts on end users by allowing developers to deal with problems as soon as they arise.
- Functional testing verifies that the program conforms to all applicable industry norms, laws, and guidelines. It confirms that the program complies with the functional, performance, security, and accessibility criteria set forth by the authorities or the industry.

7.2.1.1.1. Unit Testing

Within the more general category of Functional Testing, Unit Testing is the first sort of automation testing that we list. Software testing approach known as "unit testing" is primarily concerned with confirming the operation of individual software system units or components. The smallest tested component of a programme is referred to here as a unit; typically, this is a function, method, or occasionally a class. Unit testing seeks to verify that each code unit operates as intended by isolating and testing it independently. Before merging individual units into a bigger system, developers can quickly find and address flaws by testing the units separately. This allows for early bug discovery and fixes in the software development life cycle. Usually, developers write unit tests by creating test cases to exercise numerous scenarios. They confirm that the units behave as intended. The implementation and evaluation of unit tests are frequently automated with the use of tools and frameworks for unit testing, which improves process efficiency and manageability.

7.2.1.1.2. Integration Testing

Within the broader area of Functional Testing, Integration Testing ranks second on our list of automated test types. The purpose of integration testing, a sort of software testing, is to determine how well different software system modules, components, or subsystems connect with one another. It focuses on ensuring that the integrated system functions properly and that each component interacts with the others in the appropriate manner. Another objective of integration testing is to identify potential problems that may arise when integrating and using diverse components. It ensures that the system's many components, including as modules, classes, databases, APIs, and external systems, communicate seamlessly and produce the desired or anticipated results.

7.2.1.1.3. Regression Testing

Within the more general topic of Functional Testing, Regression Testing comes in third on our list of automated test types. Regression testing is a subset of testing for software that is used to confirm that improvements or modifications made to a programme haven't resulted in unexpected side effects or additional issues. It comprises retesting earlier verified functionality following software modifications to make sure it continues to function as intended. Regression testing seeks to identify any flaws or problems that might have been brought into the system as a result of software modifications. It aids in ensuring that any additions or changes made throughout the design process do not impact the functionality that is already in place.

7.2.1.1.4. Testing for Build Verification

It is an initial software evaluation technique that is also known as smoke testing. It evaluates whether the most important features of a new software build are functioning as intended before moving on to more thorough testing. Through this technique, major defects are found early in the development cycle, which guarantees the build's stability for additional testing. This test allows one to quickly find crucial errors and fix them before getting into more complex aspects later on in the development stage. By using this proactively strategy, you can make sure that your program runs smoothly and improves its overall level of quality. Build verification testing is an essential part of software testing that needs to be completed both prior to and immediately following the development of an application's build. Since they assist in identifying significant software issues before they affect consumers, build verification tests are an integral part of any development process.

7.2.1.1.5. Acceptance testing

Within the more general category of functional testing, acceptance testing is a subset of automation testing. One kind of functional assessment is acceptance testing. It is an important stage of software testing when the software's operational suitability and conformity with customer or sponsors' specifications and desires are assessed. Finding out if the programme satisfies the established acceptance criteria and is appropriate for acceptance or agreement by its intended consumers is the aim of acceptance testing. Acceptance Testing verifies that the software meets the required performance, accessibility, and general quality criteria as final verification before it is made available to the public.

Acceptance Testing evaluates whether the software meets established standards and functions as intended; this is analogous to the process by which students demonstrate their skills and understanding in order to acquire certificates. Acceptance testing simulates how end users will interact with the product by recreating real-world scenarios. It consists of conducting test cases designed to assess specific user interactions, organisational procedures, and operations. Reliability, efficiency, and protection are among the most important non-functional aspects.

7.2.1.2. Non-Functional Testing

Evaluating a software system's features and attributes that do not align with its functional requirements is the main objective of non-functional testing. In addition to making sure the programme works as intended, it also tries to make sure it satisfies user expectations and pertinent quality standards. It has important components that affect overall user experience, system performance, and the software's capacity to satisfy non-functional requirements. These non-functional criteria list the aspects that are essential to the software's success: the availability, speed, and adaptability, assurances, and ease of use. It involves using a variety of methods, instruments, and strategies unique to every kind of testing. It enables quick issue identification and mitigation by helping to uncover potential flaws, problems, and hazards related to non-functional features. Organizations' can improve user happiness and entire functionality of software by delivering product that not just fulfils security, efficiency, accessibility, and durability criteria but also operates correctly through Non-Functional Testing.

7.2.1.2.1. Security Testing

A crucial component of software testing is security testing, which looks for flaws, shortcomings, and possible hazards in a system to make sure it can withstand hostile attacks. Evaluating the software's capacity to safeguard confidential information, uphold data integrity, and avoid breakdowns or illegal access is the goal of security testing. The purpose of security testing is to identify and resolve security issues before they are exploited by attackers. Organizations can improve software resilience, protect personal data, and guarantee compliance with appropriate security standards and legislation by doing rigorous security testing.

7.2.1.2.2. Usability Testing

Usability testing ensures that the functioning of a product or system is accessible and user-friendly. An e-commerce website's accessibility would be tested to see if users could quickly find important content. This type of testing assesses all aspects of the user experience, such as interface usability, instructional clarity, and accessibility. Consider an e-commerce company's usability-tested purchase application. The testers are assessing the ease with which clients can conduct common tasks such as browsing and listing products, making purchase orders, deciding whether the payment gateway is user-friendly, and so on. Testers assess an e-commerce application's usability, capacity to match user needs, and interface clarity/ease of use. To ensure a positive user experience, usability testing is performed to ensure that users can interact with the software in an easy and understandable manner.

7.2.1.2.3. Compatibility testing

A software system's compatibility with other software, operating systems, or configurations is ascertained through compatibility testing. For instance, a tester makes that the programs works seamlessly and error-free with different operating systems and software programs during compatibility testing. Compatibility testing, for instance, establishes if the program functions properly across a range of operating systems and web browsers, as well as how the programme interacts with other project management tools like document-sharing or communication platforms.

7.2.1.2.4. Testing for accountability

Testing for accountability makes ensuring a system is functioning correctly. It guarantees that a given function produces the desired result. If the system yields the anticipated outcomes, it passes the test; if not, it fails. Imagine an e-commerce site where clients may browse, add products to their carts, and complete the checkout process. When a product is added, it should appear in the user's cart and be accurately recorded in the system. system to assess its stability. The reliability test will be unsuccessful if the system exhibits issues in the predetermined scenarios.

For instance, reliability testing verifies that all of an application's links and webpages function consistently and without errors, providing a trustworthy user experience.

7.3. Orientation of parts; in-bowl and out-of-bowl toolings

In-bowl toolings

In bowl-toolings are orienting mechanisms that are frequently observed in vibratory bowl feeders and other feeders with a similar design. In order to ensure that pieces are precisely orientated and positioned in advance of assembly, these instruments are essential. Pieces are oriented and aligned within a vibratory bowl feeder by In-Bowl Toolings. These instruments guarantee that parts are positioned uniformly and prepared for subsequent assembly steps.

Standard Orientation Frameworks

Wiper Blade: Common In-Bowl Tooling that softly pushes pieces along the track while preserving proper alignment is the wiper blade.

Pressure Break: Another way to manage the piece flow inside the bowl is to use a pressure break.

Slot in the Track: A design feature called a slot in the track reduces jamming and aids in part alignment.

Part-Orienting Systems Analysis

Engineers look into how well these systems work to optimize part orientation. Crucial factors to take into account are dependability, effectiveness, and simplicity of upkeep.

Out-of-bowl Tooling: As the name suggests, out-of-bowl tooling is employed in a different location than the vibratory bowl feeder. The feed track, which leads away from the bowl, uses these tooling. Pieces are certain to stay correctly orientated as they leave the bowl and move down the feed track thanks to out-of-bowl tooling. The tools and sensors known as "out-of-bowl tooling" direct and control part orientation outside of the bowl. Therefore, as parts are transferred from the bowl to the subsequent stages of assembly, out-of-bowl tooling take over, while in-bowl tooling handle the intricacies of the bowl.

7.4. Manufacturing equipment embedded with digital data

Production undergoes a digital transformation when a company starts implementing new digital technologies to enhance every aspect of the production process. The main forces behind this can be software applications and digitization, and it can be implemented in a full manner or fragmented. Big data, process optimization, and improved customer experiences are important components of factory digitization.

Examples include knowledge-based work automation, 3D printing, ERP systems, smartphone apps for front-line personnel management, and robotic process automation. Information in digital format makes it easier to exchange data, visualise processes, and interact with users via digital platforms. Moreover, using and sharing data across the digital thread would facilitate closer cooperation and deeper cross-functional integration across the whole product lifecycle, including phases involving numerous stakeholders like suppliers and customers.

The focus is shifting from optimising a single production site to numerous locations controlled by the company, its suppliers, and its end users, as well as the company itself. Industry 4.0 represents a paradigm change from the optimisation of physical assets to the optimisation of data and information used during the lifecycle of the product. A "digital thread" that functions as a digital representation of the product's lifespan and carries end-to-end information flow is the foundation of this digital optimisation. This digital thread starts with the product's digital design and continues with the digitally guided and controlled manufacturing process, digital monitoring of the finished product during use, and, at the end, digital recycling of the product, where digitally stored data can assist in identifying parts for reuse. Digital transformation in futuristic smart factory is shown in figure below.

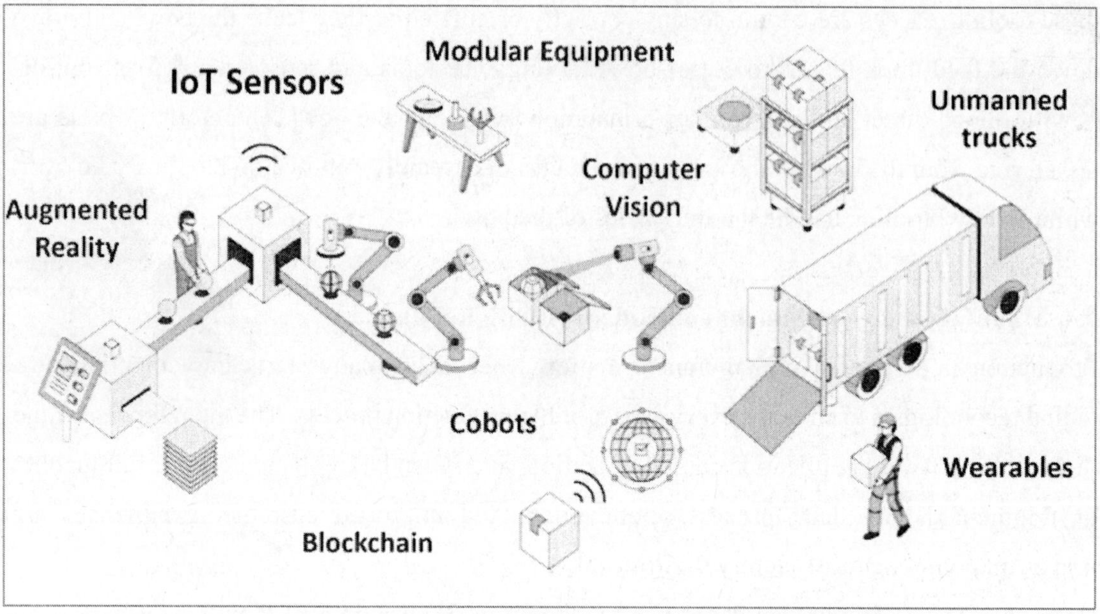

Fig. 7.2. Digital Transformation in smart factory

7.5. Manufacturing automation with autonomous decisions

The notion of autonomous production presents significant opportunities within the framework of Industry 4.0. It is imperative to underscore that the objective is not to supplant human labour, but rather to construct robust and exceptionally responsive manufacturing supply networks.

The Importance of Self-Driving Manufacturing

Resilience: To increase bottom-line performance like asset utilization and waste reduction, as well as top-line innovation and high-value commodities, manufacturing processes need to be resilient.

Adaptability: In order to deal with flexible and robust supply networks, manufacturing must be infinitely and continuously adjustable. *Change management:* When working with processes that are always changing because of variables like raw materials, process dynamics, and volume fluctuations, adaptability is crucial.

Present Automation Status: Process manufacturing has a high degree of automation that can manage both steady states and fluctuations like startup, ramp up/down, and variability. Variations in upstream processes and variations in volume/capacity demand are managed through advanced control and optimization.

Adaptive Control: The system continuously monitors, evaluates, and makes decisions in order to modify its own operation to achieve peak performance.

Closed-Loop AI for Autonomous Process Manufacturing.

Data-Driven Decision Making: New technologies allow machines to analyze massive amounts of data, detect patterns, and make autonomous judgements in real time. Manufacturing processes can be optimized, and predictive maintenance can be used.

Managing Bottlenecks: Proactive actions can help to eliminate production bottlenecks, resulting in better operational efficiency and less downtime.

Autonomous systems and artificial intelligence: Instead of taking planned moves, autonomous systems learn dynamically from their surroundings. These systems adopt and execute strategies depending on environmental cues, promoting flexibility and resilience.

To summarize, autonomous manufacturing isn't about replacing humans—it's about creating flexible, responsive, and adaptive systems that flourish in a continuously changing environment.

UNIT SUMMARY

This unit covers the fundamentals of understanding pick and place robots, testing and sorting-based systems, component orientation, and in-bowl and out-of-bowl toolings. It also reflects the factory automation strategies used in the self-driving production process.

Solved Examples

1. How do Pick and Place Robots work?

Ans1. Industrial robots called pick and place robots are made expressly to move goods from one place to another. These robotic systems are an essential part of many production and manufacturing lines because they automate jobs that are time-consuming, repetitive, and possibly dangerous, like:

- Arranging
- Classifying
- Setting

One of the most significant developments that has greatly aided in the development of industrial robotics is the pick-and-place robot. These robots have a placement inaccuracy of less than one mm and can process up to 200 goods in a minute. Pick and place robots come in a variety of forms and capacities, but all of them are built on the same core ideas.

Programming

Robots are frequently programmed to perform a specific sequence of motions, allowing them to complete tasks with high precision and consistency. The robot's end effector, which physically interacts with the objects being moved, controls the sequence of moves.

Sensor Integration

Pick-and-place robots are typically equipped with sensors that detect the presence and location of objects in their environment. These sensors may include vision systems, force sensors, and proximity sensors, among others. The data collected by these sensors is used to guide the robot's movements and guarantee that objects are picked up and placed correctly, even if their placement differs somewhat from what was projected.

2. Define briefly Smart Robots with Sensing and Vision Systems

Ans2. Robots with improved sensing capabilities were introduced in the 1980s and 1990s, enabling them to interact with their environment more successfully. These robots were equipped with force sensors, vision systems, and other technologies that allowed them to recognise objects and adjust their movements in response. It was a substantial breakthrough in the field of pick and place robotics, enabling them to carry out tasks with increased precision and adaptability.

The advancement of pick and place robots was spurred by the following factors: The creation and integration of sensors is one example of technological advancement. Robots that are stronger and lighter are the product of advances in material science. The creation and

integration of sensors is one example of technological advancement. Robots that are stronger and lighter are the product of advances in material science. Motions may now be performed more quickly and precisely thanks to advancements in motor technology. Robots may now easily do complex tasks because to advancements in computer technology that enable sophisticated control algorithms.

3. How Does the Industrial Internet of Things (IIoT) Work?

Ans3. Manufacturing is the process of utilising both human labour and machinery to produce a wide range of commodities. A range of digital technologies have been used by industry in recent decades, progressively decreasing the need for human intervention in industrial processes. Smart manufacturing is an industrial sector supported by new technologies and based on intelligent automation, which has gained popularity among many organisations. Leading digital trends in manufacturing now in play: The Internet of Things is made up of devices and sensors that are network-connected and gather vital data to enhance and simplify industrial processes. AI and machine learning are strong algorithms that process unprocessed input and provide useful outputs.

Robotics: Industrial robots have long coexisted with human labour in various industries. They are incredibly cost-effective and contribute to the generation of efficiency at every stage, from raw materials to final products.

Exercises

Q1. What do you mean by pick and place robots? Write down its advantages and disadvantages.

Q2. Discuss about testing and sorting based systems.

Q3. Explain briefly for parts orientation; in-bowl and out-of-bowl toolings.

Q4. Describe manufacturing equipment embedded with digital data.

Q5. Discuss Manufacturing automation with autonomous decisions taken by computers based on the realistic process/machines.

Q6. Write down the significance of pick and place robots.

Q7. Differentiate between in-bowl and out-bowl orientation.

Q8. Explain the following:

Wiper Blade, Pressure Break, Slot in the Track.

Multiple Choice Questions

1. What is automated testing?

   a. Manual testing by humans

   b. Automated testing by robots.

c. Automation through tools and scripts

d. Testing without test cases.

2. Which of the following is a primary purpose of automation testing?

a. Minimising the necessity for manual testers

b. Achieving 100% test coverage

c. Enhancing test efficiency and reliability

d. Eliminating test documentation

3. What is the main advantage of automated testing versus manual testing?

a. Faster test execution

b. Reduced human error

c. Improved test coverage

d. Combination of the following

4. Which kind of testing are best suited for automation testing?

a. Unit Testing

b. Regression Testing

c. Exploratory testing

d. End-to-end testing

5. What is the primary function of Regression Testing in Automation?

a. Identify new defects

b. Ensure existing functionality functions after changes

c. Validate user requirements.

d. Ensure compatibility with various browsers

6. Robots employ hydraulic drives when

a. High torque is needed

b. High power is needed

c. The robot arm must move quickly

d. All of the above are applicable

7. The following sort of robot is best suited for pick and place activities

    a. Rectangular

    b. Cylindrical

    c. Spherical

    d. Jointed arm type

8. A robot's arm might be referred to as

    a. An actuator

    b. End effector

    c. Manipulator

    d. Servomechanism

9. Which kind of actuator produces a lot of power but is often unorganised?

    a. Electric

    b. Hydraulic

    c. Pneumatic

    d. None of the mentioned

10. A robot can be programmed using one of the following methods:

    a. Touch sensing control

    b. Continuous path control

    c. Pick and place control

    d. Robot vision control

11. Which device is most commonly linked with automation.

    a. Flexible manufacturing

    b. Robots

    c. Computer graphics workstations

    d. CNC machines

12. Select the following elements for an automated machine tool:

    a. Logic

    b. NC tape programming

c. Software

d. Workstation

13. Robot configurations include:

a. Octagonal

b. Circular

c. Square

d. Spherical shapes

14. Which technology allows a procedure to be performed without the need for human intervention?

a. Variable Motion

b. Dynamic Motion

c. Automation

d. Vibration

15. Which of the following describes the use of machinery to assist human workers in completing a task?

a. Mechanization

b. Production

c. Automation

d. Assembly

16. Which of the following is not a fundamental part of an automated system?

a. Power

b. Storage system

c. Control System

d. Instructional Program

17. In an automated system, what is necessary to drive both the process and the controls?

a. Guide wires

b. Power

c. Wheels

d. Pallets

18. What is the source of electricity in an automated system?

    a. Hydrogen

    b. Diesel

    c. Coal

    d. Electricity

19. Which is referred to as the manufacturing operation carried out on a work unit?

    a. Load

    b. Product

    c. Unit

    d. Process

20. What type of power is necessary for electric discharge machining.

    a. Mechanical

    b. Hydraulic

    c. Thermal

    d. Mechanical

21. Which devices are used to communicate the commands issued by the control unit?

    a. Hydraulic Devices

    b. Modular Devices

    c. Radiant Devices

    d. Electromechanical devices

22. How are commands often conveyed in a control unit?

    a. Hyper Signals

    b. High Voltage Signals

    c. Null Signals

    d. Low Voltage Signals

23. Which of the following requires integrating factory data with the corporate information system?

    a. Monitor operators

    b. Handle materials

c. Employee monitoring

d. Data integration across the enterprise

24. Which feature prevents human workers from getting too near to the system?

a. Monitoring packages

b. Monitoring storage space

c. Monitoring errors

d. Monitoring safety

25. Which type of control is used to adjust the speed of a motor?

a. On-off control

b. Servo control

c. Proportional control

d. Integral control

KNOW MORE

For more information related to this topic scan the QR code,

OR

Type this link in your browser

https://ufile.io/im605s8j

References

1. Mikell P. Groover, "Automation, Production Systems and Computer Integrated Manufacturing" Fourth Edition, Pearson. USA. 2015.
2. https://archive.nptel.ac.in/courses/112/106/112106298/
3. https://onlinecourses.nptel.ac.in/noc21_mg83/preview

CO PO ATTAINMENT TABLE

Course outcomes (COs) for this course can be mapped with the programme outcomes (POs) after the completion of the course and a correlation can be made for the attainment of POs to analyze the gap. After proper analysis of the gap in the attainment of POs necessary measures can be taken to overcome the gaps.

Table for CO and PO attainment

The data filled in the above table can be used for gap analysis

Course Outcomes	Expected Mapping with Programme Outcomes *(1- Weak Correlation; 2- Medium correlation; 3- Strong Correlation)*											
	PO -1	PO-2	PO-3	PO-4	PO -5	PO -6	PO -7	PO -8	PO -9	PO-10	PO -11	PO-12
CO-1												
CO-2												
CO-3												
CO-4												
CO-5												
CO-6												

INDEX